101 Ways to Buy a House

*If Your Goal is to Catch a Cheetah,
You Don't Practice by Jogging*

James C. Clinkscales

iUniverse, Inc.
Bloomington

101 Ways to Buy a House
If Your Goal is to Catch a Cheetah, You Don't Practice by Jogging

Copyright © 2012 by James C. Clinkscales

All rights reserved. No part of this book may be used or reproduced by any means, graphic, electronic, or mechanical, including photocopying, recording, taping or by any information storage retrieval system without the written permission of the publisher except in the case of brief quotations embodied in critical articles and reviews.

The views expressed in this work are solely those of the author and do not necessarily reflect the views of the publisher, and the publisher hereby disclaims any responsibility for them.

iUniverse books may be ordered through booksellers or by contacting:

iUniverse
1663 Liberty Drive
Bloomington, IN 47403
www.iuniverse.com
1-800-Authors (1-800-288-4677)

Because of the dynamic nature of the Internet, any web addresses or links contained in this book may have changed since publication and may no longer be valid. The views expressed in this work are solely those of the author and do not necessarily reflect the views of the publisher, and the publisher hereby disclaims any responsibility for them.

Any people depicted in stock imagery provided by Thinkstock are models, and such images are being used for illustrative purposes only.

Certain stock imagery © Thinkstock.

ISBN: 978-1-4697-5821-3 (sc)
ISBN: 978-1-4697-5822-0 (hc)
ISBN: 978-1-4697-5823-7 (e)

Library of Congress Control Number: 2012901945

Printed in the United States of America

iUniverse rev. date: 3/1/2012

Contents

Way # 1: Kiddie Condo Loan 1
Way # 2: Pre-foreclosure 5
Way # 3: Loan Assumption and Agree to Pay. 8
Way # 4: Take Title Subject to 11
Way # 5: Release of Liability 11
Way # 6: Price to control. 12
Way # 7: Cash to control 12
Way # 8: No Doc. 18
Way # 9: Low Doc 18
Way # 10: 80% Conventional 18
Way # 11: 90% Conventional 19
Way # 12: 95% Conventional 19
Way # 13: 80% Borrow one half down 20
Way # 14: FHA $50,000 or less. 23
Way # 15: FHA More than $50,000. 24
Way # 16: VA. 26
Way # 17: Lease Option 28
Way # 18: Lease Purchase 29
Way # 19: Cash. 31
Way # 20: PMM Purchase Money Mortgage/Seller takes back a second. 32
Way # 21: 100 Year Lease 32
Way # 22: Land Contract/Installment Sale Contract/Contract for Deed 34

Way # 23: REO Real Estate Owned (bank department) 37
Way # 24: Single Payment Note/Borrow from CD 37
Way # 25: Clout Loan. 39
Way # 26: Bank vs Bank. 39
Way # 27: SAM Shared Appreciation Mortgage (bank). 40
Way # 28: SAM Shared Appreciation Mortgage (private) 40
Way # 29: Up His Appreciation. 40
Way # 30: PAM Pledged Account Mortgage 43
Way # 31: Straight Note / Straight Loan 45
Way # 32: Rule of 72 46
Way # 33: Partial Sale. 47
Way # 34: Seller Excitement Loan 48
Way # 35: Rule of 78 48
Way # 36: Transfer Account Loan 48
Way # 37: Buy-Down 49
Way # 38: Bank Stock Purchase Loan. 49
Way # 39: Company Interest-Free Loan 55
Way # 40: Swing / Bridge Loan 56
Way # 41: Neal Boortz Saving Plan 56
Way # 42: Wrap-Around Mortgage. 58
Way # 43: Magic Wrap 59
Way # 44: Low Interest Mortgage Discount 59
Way # 45: State Housing Agency Loan 60
Way # 46: "Funny" Way 62
Way # 47: Pledge Future Income 62
Way # 48: Security Deposit Loan 64
Way # 49: Put up the Car. 64
Way # 50: Tap the Insurance 65

Way # 51: Certificate of Deposit in Lieu of Discount. 65
Way # 52: Credit Union Loan. 65
Way # 53: Seller Borrow Own Equity 65
Way # 54: ARM Adjustable Rate Mortgage. 67
Way # 55: ROM Roll Over Mortgage 69
Way # 56: VRM Variable Rate Mortgage 69
Way # 57: RRM Renegotiable Rate Mortgage 69
Way # 58: FLEX Flexible Payment Mortgage (Variable Rate). . . . 70
Way # 59: GPM Graduated Payment Mortgage 71
Way # 60: LPM Level Payment Mortgage 71
Way # 61: Fannie Mae Plans: Plan 1 73
Way # 62: Plan 2 73
Way # 63: Plan 3 73
Way # 64: Plan 4 73
Way # 65: Plan 5 73
Way # 66: Plan 6 73
Way # 67: Plan 7 73
Way # 68: Plan 8 73
Way # 69: GPAM Graduated Payment Adjustable Mortgage. . . . 74
Way # 70: FLIP Flexible Loan Insurance Program 74
Way # 71: FPM Flexible Payment Mortgage 74
Way # 72: Urban Rehabilitation Program 75
Way # 73: Cut Gems 75
Way # 74: Programs 77
Way # 75: Trade Stock 77
Way # 76: RAM Reverse Annuity Mortgage 77
Way # 77: Absolute Auction 78
Way # 78: Advance Payments Deposit 78

Way # 79: Equity Advance 78
Way # 80: Guaranteed Sales Plan 79
Way # 81: Balloon Note 80
Way # 82: Blanket Mortgage 80
Way # 83: Package Mortgage 81
Way # 84: Flexible Fixed Rate Mortgage 81
Way # 85: Move A House To Your Lot 84
Way # 86: Adobe 84
Way # 87: FHA 234 85
Way # 88: Existing Condo and 203 b 85
Way # 89: FHA/VA Combo Loan 85
Way # 90: Sleaze-Bag Tax FIFA 86
Way # 91: Outbid at Foreclosure 86
Way # 92: Weekly and Bi-Weekly Mortgage 87
Way # 93: Government Bonds 87
Way # 94: Annuity (Life insurance) 88
Way # 95: Sam (Builder) 89
Way # 96: RPM Rapid Payoff Mortgage 89
Way # 97: FNMA Refinance 89
Way # 98: Duplex 89
Way # 99: GEM Graduated Equity Mortgage 91
Way # 100: Zero Interest Financing 91
Way # 101: Give Items of Value 91

Dedication

I dedicate this book to God and his Glory. He has kept me and my family safe and healthy all these years. Our kids love each other, and the cousins love and play with each other—with the birth of our first great- granddaughter, Harper, there are now twenty- two of us and we are so fortunate. For some reason, He wanted me to do this book. It's not that I needed to chase any more Cheetahs, we have ours, but, somewhere out there, someone needs a Cheetah in his life and God wants him/you to catch one or two. May you succeed! Also, this book is dedicated to my wife, Pilar. She lived with me through all these experiences, putting up with me and loving me. She is the artist who did the Cheetahs. She is a nationally known wildlife artist. I didn't teach her anything. I went to Spain on an exchange scholarship (University of Madrid) and found her. She taught me how to say Sí. I have been saying it ever since. Next year, January 28, we will have been roommates for fifty-two (52!) years! (2012)

Also, this book could not have been possible without my thousands of students, to whom this book is also dedicated. So perchance you are why He wanted me to write this book. When I got into real estate there was no training. May this little book give you some training. My training was a poem: "Welcome, James. Here's your desk. There's the phone. Go git 'em, boy. You're on your own." Whatever your profession in life, as you travel toward point "Z," there are some Cheetahs running around. Go git 'em! You're not on your own!

Introduction
by James C. Clinkscales

During the past thirty-three years, I have sold and bought real estate and taught real estate courses, including appraisal classes, to thousands of students and now I wish to take the mystique out of the whole process of real estate finance for the entrepreneur, the purchaser, the seller, the student. There is nothing more simple than the structuring of the financial part of house-buying. The easy part is finding, and allowing someone to okay a purchase agreement/sign the contract. Once upon a time, when your grandparents, uncles and aunts wanted to purchase a house, farm, place, they either paid cash, or they went to the bank and took out a loan called a straight note, or straight loan, which meant that for five years, they would pay interest only and then, when the note became due, they paid off the entire loan and the last interest amount. "Straight Note" was the only game in town. There were no other ways to finance. Amortization didn't exist. Yes, refinancing did exist. If a fellow couldn't pay off the entire amount, he could usually go the refinance route. FHA, VA, Conventional Financing as we now know it, FNMA (Fannie Mae) didn't exist. Housing wasn't so expensive, as it is now. There was very little government intrusion into people's affairs, no big utility bills, people bought a load of coal or firewood for their heating and cooking, there were no large car payments, etc. to worry about, most moms made their own clothes and most of the clothes for the kids. You got a new pair of shoes each fall to wear to school and to church, and went barefooted during the spring and summers. I mentioned church. Most people back then, went to church, the main social event of each community. They prayed for rain to make the crops, to be able to pay the mortgage. There were no televisions, few movie theatres. For diversion, I remember that people sang. Yes, you would go visit a neighbor and both families ended up singing around the pump organ or piano before you left for home. Well, back to real estate finance history.. It just so happened in the late twenties and early thirties (nineteen hundreds) that the weather changed to become a huge dry spell—probably the cows and livestock, horses, etc., were causing global warming! Crops failed. Dust blew from Texas to Georgia and back. They called it the "dust bowl" effect. At about this same time, the stock market crashed, sending the already weak economy into a "great depression." People couldn't make good on their note payments, neither interest nor principal. The foreclosures began. Why didn't people just refinance? Because, banks didn't have any money, either. Hard times! Words like "hobo," "vagabond," came into being. "Soup kitchens, soup lines." Boxcars were full of men looking for work, any sort of work, to be able to take care of their families. I remember (we were now into the second world war.) hobos coming to our back door, begging for a meal (Dad was a Baptist preacher). We later learned that it was the practice of hobos to mark the preachers' homes in each town, where a meal would be likely. Mom would fix them a plate, usually consisting of "pot liquor" and corn bread, maybe some "greens, in fine, they got the same thing we ate. You don't know what pot liquor is? It's the juice you get from cooking turnip greens! I always sat with them on the back steps and watched them eat. They were fascinating to me. Then another one would show up, smelling just like the last one. We seemed to always have "plenty." If we asked for a second helping, sometimes, Mom would say "you've had plenty." Earlier, when my mom and dad were in college in Birmingham, Alabama, (the Howard College, now Samford University), they told of always having three meals a day: Oatmeal, Cornmeal, and Skip-a-meal! Back to Finance.

    Something had to be done to put people back into housing. A fellow named J.P. Morgan had already bailed out the entire US government with his own private funds. Can you imagine that happening today? What did they do? Why, they invented FHA (Federal Housing Authority). The name that finally stuck and along with it, amortiziation. Amortization is derived from a Latin word meaning to kill-off little by little. Don't try that with a dog. To "bob" a dog's tail, one must cup off the entire tail at once. To amortize would eventually kill the dog! Also, FHA doesn't mean Future Homemakers of America, which is what I thought when my "Realtor" asked me how I wanted to "go," FHA, VA, or Conventional, meaning, of course, how I wanted to pay for the house, now that we had located it. I could not see how the only FHA that I knew about, (Future Homemakers of America—teaching little girls how to cook, had anything to do with our buying a house. My wife could already cook circles around anybody. VA? Some sort of a disease? I wanted nothing to do with that one! You see, the general public hasn't always been aware of the terms that we in the industry take for granted. I opted for Conventional, thinking myself a rather conventional fellow, or course, when it was finally explained to me that I couldn't afford "Conventional," we finally "went" FHA. My agent should have determined how we were "going" before ever putting us into his car. All professionals do that now. FHA is given credit for "amortization," which I will explain later, for putting America back into affordable housing, establishing a national building code, and thus improving the quality of dwellings in America.

This book is for anyone and everyone who wants to own the American Dream, home ownership. I have tried to keep it simple enough so that the uninformed can use it and become successful and pick up enough knowledge along the way to be very informed. There are technical parts of the book that are also kept simple. It has always been my style, inside and outside the classroom, to be funny. I like funny. I like it more than not funny. I have found that if my lectures are funny, the class enjoys the material; they leave the classroom at the end of my lecture not realizing that they have been lectured to. They thought they had been entertained. If I am having fun, then they are having fun and are learning, my whole intent in the first place. There are many other books on real estate finance that, frankly, even other real estate instructors don't even enjoy. So, over the years, I have found that real estate can be made as simple as it really is and can be enjoyable for the student. I will therefore try to make this unfunny material as fun as possible as we journey through the store with the student. Oops! I used the word "student" twice! Well, we are all students in the sense that we learn something new, so if I call you students along the way, it's from habit, having taught real estate students for over thirty years.

One doesn't have to be a mathematician to enjoy real estate finance. You would think that trigonometry, geometry, algebra, and calculus would be useful in a finance setting. Wrong! Forget that. Real estate finance is 4th grade arithmetic. Anyway, this isn't a book on real estate finance, but on a bunch of ways to buy a house and how to chase and catch cheetahs! You don't need to be a genius to go to the store. This book just gets you in and out of the store with your purchase. You decide which purchase without pressure from any salesperson. You'll have more knowledge, ammo, than they regarding your purchase when you read this book.

Just to show you how anyone, non-mathematical, can successfully even teach real estate finance, take me for example. I never liked math. You could say I hated it. I took algebra in high school and learned that it was nothing more than memorizing formulas. I have always been good at memorization. I loved Spanish, French, German and now Arabic. I happened to grow up knowing English, Southern and Ebonics. But at Auburn University (During my first three years the school was known as API—Alabama Polytechnic Institute—Auburn),I was required to take algebra and Trigonometry. I took algebra early because I thought it was easy and I made an A. Trig, I put off till my senior year. I even complained to my faculty advisor. He said that I had to take it. I don't recall his body language at the time, but he probably touched his nose when he told me that after graduation, I would use Trig every day of my life. I teach a course called The Body Language of Selling Real Estate. We know that if a person touches one's nose while talking, he is LYING. Well to make a point, I recently got out my HP_12C calculator, the only one to use if you are a real estate professional, and put in my graduation date, then that date at the time. Of the thousands of days since then, guess how many of those days I have used Trig? Four times and all on crossword puzzles! To finish this story….in my first Trig class, the teacher, General Crawford, asked the class of 48," How many of you have had Plane Geometry?" Forty-seven guys raised their hands. "Great," he said. "All turn to page 18 and we will begin." I hereby defy anyone to begin a Trig class on page 18. I flunked. I had a bad attitude. The second time I took the course, I still had the same attitude and flunked. Now, the third time, my wife and I had our first child, a job lined up to teach language and coach wrestling at Darlington School for boys in Rome, Georgia, a great future riding on this one Trig class with my time running out. Someone mentioned to me that trigonometry was nothing but formulas to be memorized. Oh, yeah? "Yeah! " Well, now. I can memorize. Though we didn't have calculators, (the engineers in class all used slide rules --disgusting things), I memorized enough sine, cosine, secant, to pull off a D! My proudest passing grade as, I was out on a "tangent" the entire time. Now, I do have in my family some very mathematical people, my brother, my wife, all my kids, even grandkids and especially one of my sons-in-law who graduated from Emory University-Summa Cum Laude. That's the best one. Then there's Magna Cum Laude, then Laude. I want everyone to know that I graduated from Auburn University-Thank Thee Laude! My Trig professor was probably in the rear of the auditorium saying "Laude how cum?' Now, back to the task at hand.

Just sit back and enjoy the trip through the real estate store. The "ways" aren't in any particular order, but they are numbered and indexed for your easy reference. Just skip the technical stuff and you may want to come back and read it later on as, you absorb and understand more and more.

You see, there is a lot of ignorance going on out there. A lot of confusion. There is nothing wrong with ignorance. That simply means that you don't know! I am ignorant in Japanese, though I have read *Shogun*.

So, in the following pages, I hope to erase all the confusion and take you from start to finish and perhaps get you excited about so many ways to do it that you will want to rush out and buy a house, and another, and another. Everyone needs a house!, or two or three, or four, so hold on to your seat and enjoy the ride. During the process of house-buying I will explain all the nitty-gritty, the details, the expenses, the requirements one must endure to get the job done. However, I hope to do it in such a way that it won't be boring, nor difficult, but fun. I will try to make it as easy as possible as I try to show you my philosophy- Life is too long not to have fun.

First, let's all get on the same wave length, that is, we must all know some of the basics of real estate, payments, vocabulary, etc. This book is not your typical finance book. How boring! This book is a book to show the beginner, the real estate professional, the regular Joe, the real estate teacher, how to buy a house. I don't presume to know everything, but I do know what I am talking about. Hopefully, whoever picks up a copy of this book, will find it enlightening, informative, and entertaining. Especially the entertaining. The teachers and professors that I remember most in all my academic endeavors were entertaining. I therefore remember their teachings. One exception was Art Yorra, my broker instructor. In class, Art was informative, fair, completely open (you could ask him anything and get a straight answer), he was also impressive in his dress. He commanded your attention and respect and got it. He was the consummate teacher's teacher! He was not entertaining. Hi, Art! Hope you are having Happy trails, just like Roy and Dale sang about. Your students will never forget you. Thanks. Some of the contents of this book are things that Art taught me in Broker's school some thirty years ago. He invented the "schematic," as he calls it, on prorations, the equitable dividing up of expenses by buyer and seller. But, I don't want to get technical. Though there is a lot of technical stuff in the following, you have my permission to skip it and just read the interesting stuff. You may want to come back to it later when you have a better grasp of the interesting and funny stuff. I have made it a point to keep everything simple. Easy. You see, real estate is easy and simple. There is no reason to make it hard, nor boring like most texts on the subject. It has always been my philosophy that life is too long not to have fun and enjoy. My style outside and inside the classroom has always been funny. I like funny. I have found that if I can make my lectures funny the class enjoys the material that I am trying to teach. And, when they leave the classroom at the end of my lectures, they have the feeling, well, some of them do, that they have had fun, not knowing that they have been lectured to. I must say that I used to find it frustrating and difficult to accept upon reading the comments required of real estate classes in Georgia. Out of, say, forty-eight students, forty-six will comment, what a great teacher! The other two? "Worse teacher I ever had." "He shouldn't be allowed to teach, etc." I talk to other teachers about this. They say "Don't read them." Well, I still read them and try to improve. I always study and prepare. That student also hates the staff, the room is too cold, hot, and they probably kicked their own dog upon leaving the house. I do understand that some people don't get the encouragement from their spouse, they are taking the classes at a bad timing in their lives, they are under stress, and are to be pitied.

I shall, therefore, attempt to make the unfunny material as bearable as possible and as you stroll through the store, you may find your purchase, decide on it and be able to take it home with you with the minimum of effort and problems. You also may even find a Cheetah, hidden somewhere and catch him! They come in all sizes and shapes and are a real treasure when you can grab hold of one and hang on. It depends on what one is looking for and what turns you on. I predict that you will leave this book more knowledgeable about your subject than most real estate agents you will encounter. Don't get me wrong. There is a world of truly professional agents out there and you will meet them. Can we talk? There are also some Slickees, the crook, and there are Dingalings as well. We are slowly but surely catching the crooks, the slickees. They most often end up in jail and good riddance! Dingaling makes a lot of money but never gets referrals, the life blood of any service business. My favorite dingaling story was told to me by a student. She had asked her real estate agent, whose last name was A. Ling, a question that required the agent to use her hand calculator. Ding, instead of answering the question by using her hand calculator, handed it to the customer saying "I don't know how to use this thing. Here, you do it." That's like being up on the examination table and the doctor hands you the stethoscope and says, "I don't know how to use this thing, here, you listen to yourself." At that moment, I would run down the hall, after, of course, having first secured the back part of my gown!

Then there is the Professional. You will meet her. And him. What a person. It's like finding the very best brain surgeon and you are scheduled for surgery. Everyone deserves a professional. That's the kind of student I teach. I have taught hundreds, even thousands in my over thirty years of teaching real estate and appraisal courses. Professionals are everywhere and you will recognize that person when you find him. They are worth their fee, most, even more than they charge.

So hang on, get ready to run—flat out! Get out of that right lane and ease over into the left lane, where all the action is. I hope you enjoy the ride.

I will begin with a teaser, and one of my favorite ways to buy a house. I will call this Way Number 1. I wrote this one in my first book in 1980, "How To Get The Referral/The Bible Of Prospecting." Since then, FHA has taken this idea as one of their own and even gave it a name. They call it the Kiddie Condo Loan. Two sets of parents, or three, go in together to purchase a house for their kids in their college town. Banks love this because of the doubling or trebling of the number of people responsible for payback. The house title is placed in the name of the kids, whereby they get credit for the credit buildup. The parents receive the tax deductions for the mortgage interest paid. Just in case you didn't know, the mortgage insurance (PMI/MIP) is now tax deductible. Let's say a three bedroom house, each of the two kids has his/her own bedroom. The third room is rented out to another student whose rent pays the monthly mortgage payment. At the end of four years (after graduation) the house is sold and the inflation has paid for the kids' education. The most expensive cost of college is room and board anyway. This FHA program differs from regular FHA purchases in that the down payment is only 3%, leaving a 97% loan. You see, in the regular FHA program, houses costing more than $50,000 (Cheaper houses are all in Mexico.), the down payment is 5% of the sales price less $500, making FHA purchases $500 cheaper than going 95% Conventional. In FHA, houses that cost $50,000 or less, if you can find one, the down payment is 3% just like this special Kiddie Condo Loan program. Did I throw too much real estate technology at you? After this book you will be fluent.

I used the word Conventional. That only means that the financing isn't a government program. The two government programs are FHA and VA. FHA no longer means Future Homemakers of America, teaching little girls how to cook and sew. In real estate terms it means Federal Housing Authority and VA is not a disease but stands for Veterans Administration.

With that first one out of the way, and there are many more to come, I want to prepare my readers, you, for the main purpose of this little book, to teach you how to get to point Z from point A. You may be a real estate agent, a plumber, a day laborer, or even a grandaddy. I want you to know: "It's never too late to be what you might have been!" How profound is that? I got that out of a fortune cookie. With that truism said, and despite whatever your trade, or what you find yourself doing, which you like or dislike, we now are going to do a little exercise. I want you to actually do it. Why are you reading this book, anyway? Do what your coach says and it will turn you into a winner. It won't take long, and, yes, I know you are anxious to get on with the "ways" to buy houses, but since we all already live somewhere, we can take this moment to find out where we are going and not worry about where we have been or where we are..

Take a sheet of paper. Write down and number as you go, what you would really like to do or be doing one year from today. Take only ten minutes and you ought to time it with a watch. Let your mind go wild. One year from now, where would you like to be? I've got to use the word "goals," although I hate to. The word "goals" has a way of becoming a stumbling block to some people, but we have to somehow get from point A to point Z by passing point B and sidestepping points C and W. Stumbling blocks are those things you see when you take your eyes off the goal. So please bear with me. Write down even the impossible, because I'm here to tell you that nothing is. Please don't be one-sided! Write down one year financial goals, one year family goals, one year health goals, one year spiritual goals, travel, fun things. Don't write down chores like pick up the laundry, clean out the garage, etc. Those things go on another list made each night of things to do tomorrow, although I must admit that "Clean up the basement" is always on my to do list. Do you need to make up with that cousin? Uncle George? Your friend? Write it down. Do you want a nose-job? A new car? Move? Take Spanish? Get that degree? Write it down. Write forty things if you can. Stop. Your ten minutes are up. Now, take that list and prioritize. Place a 1 by the most important thing to you on the list. Then a 2, 3, etc. Now copy the top ten on the back of the paper. Don't worry about the other thirty items.

They aren't yet that important to you. Take another piece of paper. In ten minutes write down your five-year goals. Where would you like to be five years from now as concerning your family, self, finances, health, fun, spiritual, travel, etc? The reason for including all these categories is so that you don't become a flat tire. You need to be well rounded when you get to point Z. Otherwise you will be that one-sided flat tire going ker-plat, ker-plat, ker-plat, slowing you down so much you never get to point Z. Five years! Let your mind go wild. Your ten minutes are up. Stop! Now prioritize that list and write the top ten on the back. Take a three by five card and on one side write the ten or so items for your one-year destiny. On the other side do the same for your five-year destiny. Now, and this is very important. Don't show these goals to anyone! Not even your spouse! Especially not to your spouse. If you did, then you would go merrily on down the road and would let <u>her</u> worry about getting to point Z, with neither of you ever getting there.

    I told you to let your mind go wild. What you would really like to do. One lady in my classes said that she wrote down Mel Gibson. She didn't say what she would do with him. A guy had put down Jane Russell (for you youngsters, she and Marilyn Monroe were hot stuff way back when). Nothing is impossible as I have said. Your subconscious is so powerful that one day Mel Gibson could just stroll up! Your subconscious also has no sense of humor. It acts on what it is fed, no questions asked. Garbage in, garbage out, as they say. Although, we aren't putting in garbage. Now then, take your goals card with you at all times. Read it aloud once a day. Twice is even better. You will soon find your subconscious leading you toward what you wrote down. Awesome! Just think! One year! Five years! And knowing what I know, those are guarantees! But it's up to you. Another thing, those prioritized goals are not etched in stone. Some of them you will strike out, delete. That is fine. We are ever changing. You will even add things to those two lists. I can promise you that when you do as instructed, you <u>will</u> reach those aims. That's scary! Whatever you wrote down is within your reach!

    When/if you find that being a real estate agent, plumber, etc., isn't what you <u>really want to do or be,</u> that's okay. It's even great because you are traveling, well rounded to point Z. If you like plumbing, etc., you are going to be the best plumber in America.

I heard Bob Richards, one night, who was speaking on stage with Zig Zigler, both dynamic speakers. Bob Richards held two World Record Pole Vaulting Olympic championships. He cleared fourteen feet, eleven inches in 1952 and fourteen feet eleven point five inches in 1956 with a bamboo pole! Of course things are changing. We now have women who can clear eight feet, flatfooted without a pole! Bob Richards is not a big guy and he said he visits campuses and meets giants—who are doing nothing. He said that if a person puts in 10,000 hours of practice, he can become the best in the world. He said if you want to play a piccolo solo in Carnegie Hall, he would buy the first ticket, even though you don't yet even know how to hold one. Ten thousand hours of practice would make you the best piccolo player in the world. I'll buy a ticket too! Did you put that on your list?

Now that you know in what direction is point Z, let's head that way. As George Washington once said "Real estate is increasingly exceeding in value and does not lose in value." You and I know that that statement is true. The only way to lose value in real estate depends on zoning, use permits, the local commissioners, lack of discipline (crime), toxic uses and taxes. There are others. Mostly, though, real estate increases or regains its value over time. We can be rather sure that real estate values in the future will continue to increase because they aren't making any more of it! There have been periods in our heritage when real estate values went down. It did in the 70's, but the trend didn't last. The values recuperated and even exceeded what they had been. So, despite your profession, real estate "houses," is where the money is and always has been and will be. An alternative would be to write "The American Novel," or invent a "widget." Otherwise—real estate!

Here is Way Number 2. Years ago in a night pre-licensing real estate class I was teaching at Kennesaw State University, back then it was called Kennesaw State College. (Now every school in Georgia is a university.), a student in class told us the following: He and his wife then owned about 47 houses in and around Cobb County, Ga., where he lives. They buy pre-foreclosures: Way # 2. The local county newspaper publishes the "Public Record" section each Friday disclosing and advertising all the legal ads including all the foreclosures for that month. Your newspaper runs these ads too. The ads must run for four weeks. Then on the first Tuesday of the following month, the advertised property goes on sale on the court house square to the highest bidder, that being, most likely, the mortgagee, the lender. Note: Throughout this book, when I use words that end in "ee/or," such as grantor/grantee, mortgagee/mortgagor, lessee/lessor, remember that the "or" does the thing talked about. The "ee" receives that action. Just think of an acupuncture process. You have a jabor and a jabee. If there isn't a higher bidder than the advertised

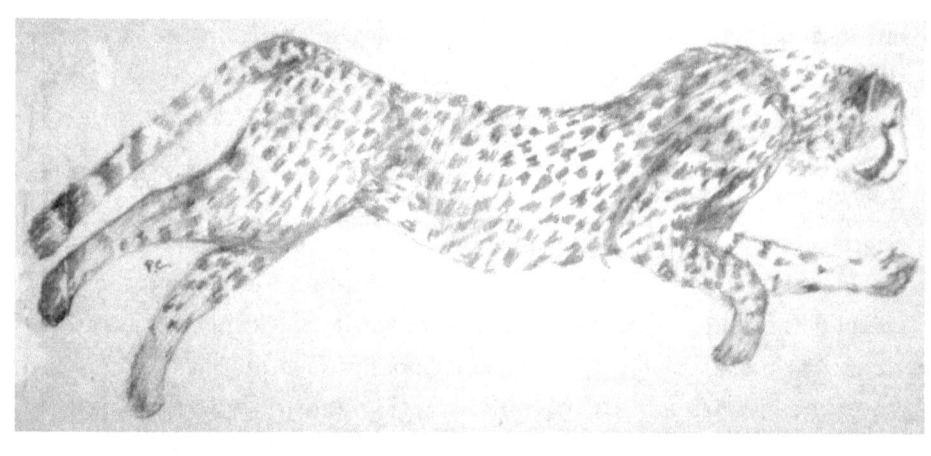

foreclosure price, the lender, one foreclosing, takes the title back and owns the house at that moment. Bid one more dollar than the mortgagee and the property is yours. The loser (for lack of a better word) has the same right as anyone else to come in and bid on his own house. On that day, he could bid in at the foreclosed price and reclaim his house. If someone bids more than the foreclosed, advertised price, and takes the house, the overage, after all expenses, goes to the one who was foreclosed upon. Let me get back to the subject. I am educating you too much! My young student told us that, generally, people will go to see the one being foreclosed on (he is in the paper) and say, "We want to buy your house." This always pleases the folks till they find out that the buyer just wants to take over payments and "to heck with you, get out of the way. You get nothing!" The ones being foreclosed do not cooperate and there is no sale. My young student told us their method: They tell the people losing their home that they would like to purchase it. (They have already decided on that house, their lawyer has already pulled a title search, making sure that there is only one lien, the first mortgage, on the property and has prepared the proper documents, loan papers and quit-claim deed as well as the title insurance.) "Here's the deal. Tonight I will write a check to your mortgage company paying all the delinquent payments, plus all the penalties and charges. The check will include three months of payments in advance for the next three months. This is a loan. Here is the interest rate. If you agree with this and can repay us in three months, we will quit-claim deed the property back to you. If you agree tonight, you will sign this quit-claim deed and the house belongs to us tonight. This is a one-time offer because of the title search. You may live in the house free for three months. Upon repaying us on this loan in three months, we will quit-claim -deed the house back to you. At that time perchance, three months will give you time to get back on your feet.

My young man said that they jump at this offer. They have three months to lie (tell) to their friends—"we sold the house." Perchance their credit is a little better off (they were not actually foreclosed upon). He told us that no one has ever paid them back! He also recommends that you never rent the house to those people! A most important fact: Their average cash outlay per house has been $7,000!

Did you like that one? More are on the way. I'm enjoying this too! Never wrote it down before. In this number 2 way to buy a house, the people move out in three months, they are friendly to you and didn't tear up the place as in most foreclosures. They even like you! You saved their skin. I used to think my young student a slickee. I soon realized that he was not taking advantage of anyone. These people being foreclosed upon had already messed up big time. Their names were already advertised in the local paper. He had nothing to do with that. He was a savior. This year of our Lord, 2007, in April, there were 447 foreclosures of homes in Cobb County. In May there were 330. In June alone there were again over 300. There are 420 foreclosures as I write. It is now 2008 and I am still writing. Folks, that's a lot of houses being taken back by the lender in just one county. This month, April of 2008, there were more than 700 foreclosures in Cobb County, Georgia. That's a lot of opportunities for the alert. My young student did tell us that his and his wife's job now is simply to read the Friday's Marietta Daily Journal. Each county has its local legal ads paper. They have trucks and crews (hope they speak English) to do all the donkey work involved in land lording.

Now I would like to take the opportunity to recommend to you a book and an author. John Adams wrote *The Landlord's Survival Guide For Georgia*. He tells you on tape/CD and in writing what to say, do, how to respond and, yes, how to survive. Most laws enacted regarding rental property are in favor of the tenant. This book includes his "Killer Lease," and the one I use and recommend. If I could not replace this book, (Mine's the 1994 version, (Yours will be newer.), I would not sell it at any price! John Adams is a local real estate investor in the Atlanta market and has a weekly talk show on a radio station. Let me show you how astute he is. Remember that in "way" number 2 the people are supposed to move out in three months? What if they don't? Court house, $94 for eviction, etc., timely appeals. Here is how John Adams handles it. Remember that these people need MONEY. John Adams said to simply show them three $100 bills. "If you can be out by Friday at four o'clock, and if the house is free and clean of debris, I'll come by and inspect, I'll give you these three $100 bills." It works every time and is worth every penny.

Now I must pause and fuss at some of you. You didn't take the time to do the little exercise that your coach asked you to do. You just kept on reading and though you found the little exercise interesting, you didn't do it! You will therefore never know nor find out where point Z is. You will also forever wander around point L (Lost) like you have been doing till now. You will get up every morning and do your best. The rest of us will get up every morning and do something! We will also catch a few cheetahs on our way to point Z. You should stop reading this little manual. I feel truly sorry for you! Shame on you! Now, go and do that little exercise and join us on a fantastic journey!

Now, here come Ways numbering three through seven—Loan assumptions. Before Jimmy Carter's fiasco (I voted for him once.), loan assumptions were common place in America. Most banks allowed them though they preferred and wanted to be able to qualify our buyers first. Basically, a loan assumption is where a buyer gives the seller his equity (amount or profit above the loan amount) and then begins making the regular monthly payments instead of the seller. There are several ways to do this, some benefiting the seller, some benefiting the buyer, and one benefiting the lender.

First of all, before you sell your house with any kind of mortgage balance due, you should send a letter to the mortgagee (bank) indicating that you plan to come in within the next thirty days and repay or refinance that loan. This is very important! If a person doesn't send that letter and just moseys into the bank to pay them off or refinance, the bank is allowed to charge you up to two months' interest penalty! This isn't what we call a prepayment penalty. By sending the letter within thirty days of repayment or refinancing, banks are disallowed to charge this fee. This is also allowed on government loans—FHA and VA, whereas, prepayment penalties are disallowed on government loans. Might as well explain what a prepayment penalty is, here. You may want to skip this technical stuff: If your loan is with Lendum and Watchem Squirm Mortgage Company at eight percent and you notice that another bank across the street has a lower rate and your bank won't match it, you then go across the street and refinance the loan at the new lower rate, your present bank, with a prepayment penalty is allowed to charge you five percent of the loan in year one, four percent in year two, three percent of your loan in year three and so on down to one percent in year five. After five years there can be no prepayment penalty. You see, the way banks make the most money is during the first years of the loan. Again, Government loans do not allow prepayment penalties. That mortgagee letter is the same one that real estate agents get you to sign when we take your listing. We are asking your mortgage company for personal information that requires your signature, is the loan assumable, mortgage balance, escrow balance, interest rate, etc. We then give you several letters for you to send one on the first of each month. Remember the up to two months' interest penalty you save? Your real estate agent is worth the money!!!

Now, back to Number 3. You should know that all contracts, loans, are assignable unless you agree that they aren't. All of them! That agreement should be in writing. In the Jimmy Carter days we began loan assumptions with a vengeance. They became the majority of our sales. Fannie Mae (Federal National Mortgage Association), who buys loans from banks weren't getting any new loans to buy. Also, with there being so many loan assumptions going on, they weren't getting the cheap money back so they could sell it for higher interest rates. I already said that the national interest finally reached 21%!!!, which was like trying to buy three houses at one time. Excuse me! I'm still doing a lot of educational and technical stuff that you might want to skip—go do that little exercise. Fannie Mae began pressuring banks to stop the loan assumptions. In compliance, banks began stamping our mortgagee letters "Not Assumable." After reading "Not Assumable," we would get the seller's loan papers and find that the bank had lied. There was nothing in the loan papers precluding an assumption/assignment, so we went ahead and arranged the loan assumption. Loans were being assumed and reassumed and reassumed. We even wrapped mortgages—I'll tell you about wrap-around mortgages later. We had to make a living and keep the American Dream alive, didn't we? In case you didn't know who is Fannie Mae, her sister is Ginnie Mae and they both mess around with Freddie Mac.

It's a long story and technical, but I'll simply say that Fannie Mae finally won the battle threatening Georgia that if we didn't start including Paragraph 17 (Due on Sale Clause) in our loan papers, she would cease buying loans from Georgia. We capitulated immediately. I'll also tell you about paragraph 17 later. Bet you can't wait!

Way Number Three. A <u>regular</u> loan assumption is where you assume the seller's loan and <u>agree to pay it</u> (the loan), called assuming and agreeing to pay. This benefits the seller because in case of a foreclosure, you didn't pay as agreed, the seller's name is foreclosed and advertised. You lose the house which goes to the bank or to the highest bidder. If that foreclosure harmed the seller (he got foreclosed on), he may sue you for not paying as agreed.

Way Number Four. This is a loan assumption, same as all of them—buyer gives the equity to the seller and begins to take up (pay) payments in lieu of the seller, however this one is called Taking Title Subject To…..(the loan). The buyer didn't <u>agree</u> formally to repay the loan. Oh, he must repay or lose his house in foreclosure proceedings, but in this case, since he didn't agree to pay, the seller, whose name is advertised in the foreclosure, can't sue the purchaser if he were harmed in the foreclosure.

Way Number Five. This assumption is called Release of Liability. The bank loves this one which also benefits the seller. The buyer must jump through the same hoops originally required of the seller and if qualified, they then remove the seller's name from the mortgage. Any subsequent foreclosure proceedings would be in the name of the purchaser. Of course, this loan assumption is rather ridiculous because if the buyer could qualify, he could just as easily buy the house with a new loan. A loan assumption does, however, save that low interest rate, there is no origination fee, no discount points, no new escrow, etc. and the closing costs would only include the limited title search, lawyer fees, and instead of thousands of dollars, a mere under $500. The purchaser simply buys the seller's escrow account, doesn't order a new survey unless he wishes to spend the money and likewise, saves on an appraisal that banks always require. Whereas regular loans take around six weeks to do, a loan assumption can take place within a week.

In all of the above loan assumptions there are two "wrinkles," if you will, that must be mentioned and since I think them so important, I'll use up two "Ways" with them. In these two instances, I am going to name two agents by name—The Pro and Ding-a-ling. First of all, the Pro—the professional real estate agent knows how to and does keep the seller and buyer aware of the exact loan amount. We have rate books and calculators that are easy to use. Ding-a-ling doesn't know how to use either! With a professional writing the contract there is a clause included in the contract that says *Price to Control,* using up Way Number 6. This means that the purchaser, at closing, will pay the seller the difference between the actual loan amount and the sales price. Duh! I thought that that is what a loan assumption is! Well, not always. Enter Ding-a-ling. When the agent first listed the house she/he sent the mortgagee letter as always. However, months have passed and the loan balance is no longer, say, $60,000. It is now $59,500, but the agent neglects to advertise the new balance and if the asking price is $100,000, under the advertised equity of $40,000, the purchaser says "I'll give you your $40,000 and the sales price will be approximately $100,000—*Cash to control,* and Way Number 7. Cash to Control must be written in the contract. The professional (Pro) knows how. Here I must say that agents may be legally on the side of the seller or on the side of the buyer. In whichever case, the agent looks out for his man by inserting Cash to Control, Price to Control, Assume and agree to pay, Take title subject to...etc. Your Agent is worth it!

But! You say loan assumptions are no longer possible?? Wrong again!! They're back!!!! Yes, but, what about paragraph 17 that you sign that says this loan may not be assumed without written permission from the lender? Well, let me tell you about a Cheetah coming up in these next few lines. Entrepreneurs, buyers, investors, everybody, enjoy! I learned this from John Adams on one of his radio shows. All loans, yes, ALL loans are now assumable. They always have been despite paragraph 17 and all the documents that you signed, the due on sale clauses, etc. All loans may be "assumed." Here's how it works. Say, John Jones wants to sell his house to you, and he has an attractive mortgage, low interest, etc. Remember Way No 2, buying pre-foreclosures? You take up payments on the seller's loan. Well, the lender may foreclose on you/him. Not anymore. Mr. John Jones gives a "limited power of attorney" to you. You are now legally John Jones. The limited power of attorney gives you, the new "John Jones" the authority to deal with his mortgagee/bank in any way and any manner that he would deal with them. Powers of attorney are legal documents in America. If one has power of attorney from someone, they are called an attorney in fact. They/you are now legally able to do whatever it was that the power bestowed upon you to do, sign a certain document, make whatever decision, etc. So, since you are now legally "John Jones" to deal with that mortgage company in any way he would, there isn't a thing the mortgage company can do about it. You (John Jones) are now paying the mortgage. That is not a loan assumption. It is, but it is not. Nothing has changed. John Jones is still paying his mortgage. One note of caution, all powers of attorney dealing with real estate transactions must be recorded. Don't forget that detail. Also, don't forget "limited" power of attorney. Important: a power of attorney may only be given by someone capable of contracting, age wise, in his right mind, and capable. That means that so long as the original John Jones is alive, the limited power of attorney is valid. They can't foreclose. You have to keep praying for the original John Jones to stay in capable health. How about that, troops? Isn't that fantastic? So, when you have your attorney draw up the quit-claim-deed, do the title search, title insurance, etc., as in # 2, also have him draw up a Limited Power of Attorney. That was a cheetah, agreed?

Time out!

At the time of typing these pages, there is history being made. It is August of 2007. Barry Bonds just broke Hank Aaron's home-run record! The person who caught the ball, supposedly worth one half million dollars, has already received a bill from IRS. Shame on America for putting up with such an organization! They want money! He only has a leather ball and he says he would like to keep it. Were I he who caught the ball, I'd cut out that percentage chunk from the ball that they claim and send it in to the U.S. Treasury. Let them have their piece of it! Can you imagine the millions it would take to reunite the two pieces? Just thinking… I already told you a little about buying pre-foreclosures. Here's another one to think about while I'm on the subject of IRS. This happens often and you didn't know it was going on. A person owed, say, a $200,000 mortgage. The bank, because he is behind on payments, forecloses and takes back the house. However, at the foreclosure sale the house only brings in to them only $125,000. This means a shortfall of $75,000 for the bank. Since they got the man's house back, the bank then, bless their hearts, forgive the man the $75,000. IRS sends him a bill, claiming the taxes on the $75,000 as income to him! IRS calls that one a 1099 Shortfall! Shame on the United States of America for putting up with such an organization! As for Barry Bonds, he doesn't respect himself so why should I? One night at the Atlanta Stadium, my wife and I saw Barry play. He played left field. A fly ball was hit that would fall just behind second base. Barry's teammates, the second baseman and the center fielder were standing there to catch the fly ball. Barry bonds runs all the way from left field, runs in front of them and catches the out! The two teammates just look at each other as if to say "What a jerk! Bless his heart." You see, here in the South you can badmouth anyone as much as you like so long as you say "Bless his heart," afterwards.

Not through with history. The day after tomorrow will be Labor Day. Here in Marietta we have a 10K road race. A Kenyan will win it. Those of us who have read Robert Roark's *Something Of Value*, know why Kenyans always win those races. In Kenya, the little boys are trained as warriors. Part of their training is running. A group of them will run twenty miles to get a drink of water! Then they run back. The winner will be a member of the Kikuyu, the Masai, or the Zulu tribe. I am impressed. They have found out that we Americans will give them trophies and money just for running down the road.

Now, let's get back to buying houses, etc. To update the previous foreclosure report—in August, in Cobb County alone, there were 439 foreclosures. In October—an update—there were 698 foreclosures, Cobb County! We had as many as 672 foreclosures in a recent month in Cobb County alone, averaging 600 each month for a while, as I already added, over 700 foreclosures in April, 2008. If you can't make a deal with that many choices, you need to keep your day job.

Technical time. Now that you know a few ways to buy a house we need to mention how to take title—my name, her name, or both? Real estate agents aren't allowed to tell you how to take title because that would be practicing law. Our typical answer and the one required by real estate license law: "You need to consult an attorney to determine how to take title." We typically don't answer in that manner, because who wants to consult another attorney? We tell them that there will be an attorney handling the closing and you can ask him. Here is his number. The typical educated adult should know the following basics. If there is only one name on the deed, that is called ownership in "severalty." That sounds like a misnomer, severalty. Sounds like several. Not. It means severed from all, single and sole ownership and at the owner's death the property will go to that person's heirs, or to whomever their will indicates. Do you know what a will is? It's a dead giveaway! If one dies without a will, he has died unwillingly! There is a legal name for that situation, though and it is "intestate," dying without a will. We sing about it every year at Christmas time: "No will,,no will,,no will, no will. Born is the King......" well, we spell it differently: Noel. The worse thing a person can do to his spouse is to die intestate, at least in Georgia. When two or more people have their names on the title, they are said to have concurrent ownership. There are several of these and each state may be different. In Georgia, if there are two names on the deed with nothing else said or requested, the two people will own the property as "tenants in common." That is a legal kind of co-ownership with inheritance rights. The owner's legal heirs receive that person's share of the property. You see why a will is imperative. All concurrent ownership comes with undivided ownership. That means that if there are four owners, each owns one forth undivided from the whole. Say, there are four owners owning a piece of property of which one forth is a swamp. Three of them can't tell the fourth owner "We didn't rent out the swamp. The swamp is yours. You get no money." Not! The entire property is undivided. Each of the four should receive one fourth of the rents. One of them dies, his one fourth goes to his heirs or assigns.

Another concurrent ownership is called Joint Tenancy, with right of survivorship. This means that, say, there are six owners of a piece of property. They each own one sixth. One of them gets run over by a bus. The other five are automatically vested in one fifth of the property. A second gets run over by a bus. Immediately and without any fanfare, the "survivors" are vested in one fourth of the property, automatically. A third owner gets run over by a bus. Again, each survivor now owns one third of the property. And, yes, a forth owner gets run over by a bus. Again, each survivor now owns one half of the property, no questions asked. However, if one of these gets run over by a bus, there's an investigation!

Another concurrent ownership is called "tenancy by the entireties." This type ownership is not recognized in Georgia, but is automatic in some states, just like tenancy in common is automatic in Georgia unless you request otherwise. Tennessee is one of those states. You must ask your attorney about your particular state. Tenancy by the entireties is, as I understand it, a husband/wife type of Joint Tenancy, probably looking out for the young couple who have no written will.

Here is something "slick" for you entrepreneurs that you might like. I said slick, not slickee! My attorney said that this was legal, not illegal. Georgia has a unique deal, or perchance it is a county thing, in which if you are a property owner, upon reaching the age of 62, you can apply for an exemption on the school taxes, which is most of your property tax bill. If you are the owner of your property and your spouse turns 62 first, then quit-claim-deed the house to that spouse. You're supposed to trust your spouse, right? The now owning spouse can exempt the school taxes. If you are concurrent owners, same thing. Quit-claim-deed the house to that person. Here comes the "slick" part. At the same time

you quit-claim-deed the property to your spouse, have your spouse at the same time quit-claim-deed the house back to you. You record the other one and keep the latter one in your safe place. This has nothing to do with trusting your spouse, but very prudent, saving probate/will expenses, etc. And, should a tragedy occur, Heaven forbid, all you need do is record that quit-claim-deed.

An added note to Way Number One, remember the Kiddie Condo Loan? The property is placed in the name of the kiddies for their benefit and is part of the program. Well, at the same time, so that you will always be in control, have kiddies sign you a quit-claim-deed. Never know what the kiddies may do with title to a house….just thinking! Did you like that one? There may have been a Cheetah in there for some of you! I have told attorney investor friends the above and especially that part in Way #2, buying pre-foreclosures about "powers of attorney," and they thought that was brilliant! Wishing they had thought of it.

It is time for Way Numbers 8 through 12, Conventional.

Conventional isn't hard. It only means that it isn't government. There are two main govt. loans and they are FHA and VA or GI loans. First of all, and foremost in any sort of loans, the underlying theme is: What is the risk for the lender. Briefly, and beginning with the least risk is the No Doc. Loan, meaning no documentation required. In essence, this loan is a signature loan. You walk right in, sit right down and they give you a loan. The only thing you have to do is wait the 24 hours (rescission period) to be over. To get this loan, one must put down payment, depending on the bank, more than 25%. The property is worth 100%. If the lender must foreclose, they get the whole house, thus not losing, so to speak—Way Number 8.

Way Number 9: called the low Doc., or Low Documentation loan. Here one pays a down payment of at least 25%, again, depending on the bank. Not much risk here with the house's being worth 100%, foreclosure would mean that the lender is in rather good position.

Way Number 10: The 80% Conventional loan. Here the buyer puts a down payment of at least 20% of the value and the lender will lend the balance. Of the three Conventional basic loans, 95%, 90%, and 80% loans, this one has the least risk for lenders. Although there are foreclosures here, people will rarely walk away from 20% of themselves, and if so, the lender claims 100% of the house.

Way Number 11: The 90% Conventional loan, of course, is where the borrower makes a down payment of 10% and the lender lends 90%. Duh! However, it has been proven that people will walk, not run, away from ten percent of themselves, hence foreclosures. To lessen this risk and loss, in case of foreclosure, the bank charges "Mortgage insurance," called P.M.I., Private Mortgage Insurance, an insurance policy in case of foreclosure that pays the loss-payee/lender if, at foreclosure, the property should sell for less than 80% of the value. This in essence, places the risk at the same level as the above 80% loan and the borrower pays for the insurance policy.

The cost of this P.M.I. insurance is 2% of the loan amount, paid at closing. That pays for the risk for the life of the loan, namely, for ten years, as the risk lessens as inflation increases, hence P.M.I. policies are for ten years or less. There are times when P.M.I. will refund money when the risk is gone (during times of good inflation/rising values) in the real estate market. If one wishes, he may finance part of the P.M.I. each year. To do this, at closing on a 90% Conventional loan, he pays a down payment on the insurance policy of ½% of the loan at closing and includes in his monthly payments for ten years or less, an amount equal to Loan times .0025 (1/4%), divided by 12: 1/12 of ¼% of the loan. This is called by the real estate industry "spreading the P.M.I." I am told by students that P.M.I (The insurance company) is very good at notifying borrowers when to discontinue these monthly payments. One other thing, the borrower must qualify for this additional monthly charge added to his payments, of course.

Way Number 12: The 95% Loan. Of course, one makes a down payment of 5% of the value and the lender lends 95% of the value. Here's where most of the foreclosures occur in the Conventional Loan Category. People will skedaddle from 5% of themselves, so, of course, there is fore-closure insurance, P.M.I. Again, P.M.I. is insuring the loan that, in case of foreclosure, and at the foreclosure sale, the property falls below 80% of the value, the policy kicks in and pays the mortgagee, all at the expense of the borrower, who paid for the policy. In the 95% loans, the cost of P.M.I. at closing is 2 ½ % of the loan. This pays for the entire P.M.I. foreclosure insurance. Or, the borrower can "spread the P.M.I." by paying down 1% of the loan at closing, then, as in the 90% loans: Loan times .0025, divided by 12 as the monthly insurance payment. He must qualify for these payments.

How foolish it would be to pay off the P.M.I. at closing when you can borrow the money at one quarter of one percent to spread the P.M.I. Invest the balance, after the down payment,(one and one half percent) in the bank and receive a whopping 2% if one is lucky. Remember when we used to whine and gripe about the low 5% interest passbook saving accounts? How boring all that was unless, you didn't know it before.

Here comes Way Number 13. Very few real estate agents seem to know this one. This is in regards to the 80% Conventional loan. Of

course, the borrower must put down payment of 20% of value or sales price, which-ever is the smaller. But did you know that the borrower may put down payment of only 10% and borrow the balance 10% from the seller? Cool! So long as the lender has this in writing in the sales agreement, the borrower qualifies for the 80% loan and avoids paying P.M.I! I like that one too. Almost a Cheetah! The borrower must, of course, qualify for the payments to the seller. If your agent isn't aware of this, inform him. Most haven't heard of the Kiddie Condo Loan either.

For the student who may be tested on all this, I will simplify the Conventional Loan in a schematic nutshell. For the rest of you, you may just skip this section. First of all I will form three columns:

95	90	80

These three columns represent the loan to value ratios. Example; 95% loan to 100% value, 90% loan to 100% value, etc. The bank will lend you 95% of the value or the sales price, whichever is the lower. Then:

95	90	80
2½	2	

This line represents the foreclosure insurance, i.e. PMI (Private Mortgage Insurance). 2 ½ % of the 95% loan is the price for this insurance. This foreclosure insurance insures the lender that if you get foreclosed, at the foreclosure sale, if the price should fall below 80% of the value, the insurance kicks in so that the bank isn't out so much. What PMI actually does, and at the expense of the borrower, is to convert the 95% and 90% loans into 80% loans risk-wise. Then:

95	90	80
2½	2	
1	½	

This line represents the down payment on the foreclosure policy should you wish to finance the policy rather than pay it off at closing. 1% of the 95% loan is the amount, ½ % of the 90% loan, etc. You have already noticed that there is no foreclosure insurance on the 80% loans because if they foreclose, they get 100% of the house, so the risk is negligible as far as loss to the bank is concerned.

Then:

95	90	80
2½	2	
1	½	

Loan X .0025 divided by 12.

This line represents the amount of monthly payment added to your house payment to cover the foreclosure insurance that you financed. Both 95% and 90% loans use this same formula to secure the monthly PMI. This insurance lasts for ten years or less. Yes, less in some cases. After ten years there should be no risk for the bank due to inflation. The loan to value ratio by then would be well out of line, in favor of the bank. So:

95	90	80
2½	2	
1	½	

L X .0025 div. by 12

This little schematic is all there is to know about Conventional.

I'll go ahead and get the dull stuff out of the way. FHA. Federal Housing Authority. This is a government program—there are two, VA. and FHA. VA stands for Veterans Administration or GI Loans, G.I standing for Government Issue.

There are two basic FHA loans. Granted, there are many FHA loans that don't comply with what I am about to teach you. Here are the basics. If a house is valued or costs $50,000 or less, (and they are all now in Mexico)—joke, the down payment is only 3%. $50,000 times 3% equals $1,500. And FHA will insure the balance. Yes, there is foreclosure insurance to pay for. Remember PMI, the Conventional foreclosure insurance? Well, this insurance isn't called PMI. It is called MIP. You see, the government agency was dyslexic. PMI stands for Private Mortgage Insurance. MIP stands for Mortgage Insurance Premium. There is a difference. PMI, the Conventional foreclosure insurance is for ten years or less. MIP, the government foreclosure insurance lasts for as long as the loan—the way to pay for the program.

To continue, if the house costs more than $50,000, then the down payment is 5% of the value minus $500. That makes the basic FHA purchase $500 less than a 95% Conventional loan. So, there are two basic FHA loans. Remember this is basic. Cheap houses ($50,000 or less), 3% down payment. More than that, 5% down payment less $500. Teaching this for years, the basics, I am tired of agents telling me that "No, FHA is a 97% loan!! Duh! Folks, they are referring to the many, many PROGRAMS offered by the government. Do you remember the opener, the Kiddie Condo Loan? That is a PROGRAM. I am teaching you here the basics: Cheap houses—3% down payment, etc.

Enough of the tired educational stuff. Anytime you go FHA, at closing, you will pay a one-time fee of 1 ½% times the loan. Then, forever, you will pay one twelfth of ½ % of the loan monthly (the MIP). I guess I shall call the FHA basic program Way Number 14—houses costing $50,000 or less, and houses costing more than that Way Number 15 ways to buy a house.

You may be already thinking—how much house can I afford to buy and qualify for at the bank?

A rule of thumb for How Much Can I Afford is two and one half your salary. Say, you make $100,000, you should be able to afford a $250,000 house. That is, of course, ball park. There are many other factors. Remember, this is basic finance. Then the bank will qualify you to find out your "ratios." To be very conservative, and I teach this, the bank doesn't want your payments, including principle and interest, and PMI, to exceed one fourth of your take-home: Your take-home is $2,000, then your payment should be around $500. Again, this is basic and very conservative. After that you must consider your ratios of output to income. I like for your house payment to be close to one forth of your income, or 25%. Banks will lend you a Conventional loan if your payment is up to 28% of your take home pay. You can get an FHA insured loan if your monthly payment is even up to 29%! The other ratio is your monthly payment plus any debt that would take ten months to pay off, such as car payments, alimony, insurance, etc. and living expenses—utility bills, phone, etc. Conventional loans are comfortable with this ratio not exceeding 36% of monthly take home pay. FHA insured loans like for your ratio not to exceed 41%. I personally think that the 41% ratio is nearing Foreclosureville. My opinion. So, there we have it. The Conventional ratios are 28% and 36%. FHA ratios are 29% and 41%. It is pretty easy to apply the above to your personal lifestyle. Don't count bills that may be paid off in less than ten months (some banks use six months).

VA loans are guaranteed by the government. There is no foreclosure insurance (PMI nor MIP). Instead, the qualifying for the VA loan is more strict than Conventional and FHA loans. To be eligible for a VA loan, the veteran must serve for at least a 90 day period during a designated war. The war didn't have to last 90 days! If no war, then the veteran must have served in active duty for at least two years (peacetime). Or, the veteran must have served more than six years' service in the National Guard or Reserves. The veteran has a paper called his/her DD214 (Department of

Defense paper 214). Every veteran has one. If not, just by contacting the Veterans Administration, will get that document for the veteran. Good credit is a must for obtaining a VA loan.

How much house can one buy if one qualifies? There is no limit on the price of the home for a Veteran. We will guarantee that loan even in the millions. Of course, the Veteran must qualify for the payments! FHA has a limit for each state. For example, Georgia as of late, just raised that FHA from $346,250 limit to $350,000. What a big deal! This will vary from state to state. However, in Georgia one can't "go" FHA, $350,000, in each county, and there are 159 counties in Georgia! That means we have 159 county school superintendents, etc! The maximum FHA loan in the Georgia counties depends on the SMSA (Standard Metropolitan Statistical Area)—the number of foreclosures per capita, etc. To find out how much house one can by, one needs only contact FHA or ask a local loan officer. Conventional loans also have no cap on value. The house must appraise as do all loans and the purchaser must qualify for the payments. Wow! That was too much technical stuff. Sorry. Just skip the un-cool part. I tried to make it as simple as I could. There are untold volumes written on FHA, Conventional and VA, but as it is so boring, I don't intend to include it here. Buy one of those Finance Books if you ever get insomnia!

Finally, though, and still on the same subject of qualifying for a loan or coming up with enough cash for the closing, there are several things a person may do to qualify for a loan. Sell off that extra car, eliminating that payment—brings down that ratio and gives you cash. Sell boats, campers and trailers to get cash. You guys, one of the best ways to get extra cash is to get your wife a second and third job! Like that one? One other thing, in qualifying for a loan, one must show stability. The banks want at least two years on the job. Say you are a plumber. In the past two years you changed jobs once and got a raise. You are still a plumber. That's good, or not bad. Say that you are the same plumber and changed jobs twice in the past two years and got a raise both times. That's bad! Frowned upon by the bank. You don't show stability. Twice in the last two years the collateral (house) was in jeopardy. Enough said.

It's time for Way Number 16—VA Loan. I have already pointed out the way a Veteran must qualify—time spent in the service, etc., needs great credit. While there is no limit on the value of a VA Loan, there is a maximum of the NO-Down-Payment VA Loan. We generally speak of VA loans as 100% loans as opposed to the Conventional 95% 90% and 80% loans. Just recently congress passed a bill which President Bush signed, placing the Veterans' entitlement onto the amount of a Conforming Loan that Fannie Mae would buy. That means a loan using Fannie Mae documents. Entitlement means how much Play-like money each Veteran has to use in purchasing a home. I said "home." The Veteran and the FHA purchasers must swear to live in (occupy) said home. Up until now, Congress had to convene and pass a new law each time raising the Veteran's entitlement, to keep up with inflation and the rising prices of homes. We want the Veteran to be able to live in a nice place. You multiply times four the Veteran's entitlement. At one time it was $20,000. That meant that a Veteran could purchase an $80,000 house and have no down payment. Then they raised the entitlement to $30,000. A $120,000 Home, no down payment! Then for many years $60,000 was the entitlement figure. A $240,000 home. Now Fannie Mae will purchase a Conforming loan of $417,000. That means that a Veteran's entitlement is $104,250 (one fourth of that). A Veteran, if qualified, can purchase a house whose sales price is $417,000 with no down payment. And now the VA Entitlement program is tied in with Fannie Mae. When Fannie Mae goes up, so does the Veteran's entitlement. That is wonderful. In most neighborhoods a $417,000 home is not too shabby. I have already said, though, that there is no limit on the sales price of a VA purchase. If a Veteran purchases a home that exceeds the No-Down-Payment limit, since he ran out of Play-like money, which was one fourth, he must use Real Money—one fourth. Example: The Veteran qualifies and wants to purchase a house priced at $417,400. This price exceeds the limit by $400. He now has a down payment. No, not $400!

He only must pay $100 down payment. Remember, he ran out of play-like money (entitlement) which was one fourth). Now he comes up with one fourth of real money. Say he wants to purchase a $1,000,000 house and qualifies and it appraises. Take the $1,000,000, subtract $417,000 from it. The balance is $583,000. One fourth of $583,000 is his down payment--$145,750. Is this boring, or what? For you, maybe, but for some Veterans, it might be helpful. With the present entitlement setup, a Veteran will probably never give out of entitlement. However, there are some Veterans out there who have used up some of their entitlement. Say a Veteran bought a $30,000 house years ago and sold it on a loan assumption. So long as there is any balance on that old loan, the Veteran has lost some entitlement. Formula: Take the sales price $30,000 times 60%. That equals $18,000. This Veteran has used up $18,000 of his now $104,250 entitlement. He now has $86,250 of entitlement times four. He may purchase a house valued at $345,000, no down payment. Once that $30,000 house is paid off to the last dollar, he is automatically restored the used up entitlement.

Another trick for Veterans is that they can swap entitlements. A Veteran is transferred from Atlanta to Chicago. His house is under the VA Loan program. If he sells to an incoming Veteran, and that Veteran willing, there is a paper they may both sigh swapping entitlements. The incoming Veteran takes over the departing Veteran's entitlement and the departing Veteran goes to Chicago fully entitled again. Neat!

God bless all our Veterans! They served our country, many right out of high school or college. If you think they got rich in the Service, think again. They have to pay for their own uniforms! While they are in the Service, back home, all the good-looking gals get married (guys too). So, after four years' Service, the Veteran comes home. No money. No good looking girls (guys). No fun. The least we could do is give them a pile of Play-like money to buy a house with. And that's the VA—GI Bill. The Veteran may also use the entitlement for getting an education.

One other note for Veterans: VA doesn't care where the Veteran gets his down payment—initial investment, if any, so long as it is mentioned in the original paperwork. A seller cannot take back a second mortgage at closing without VA's knowing about it in the sales contract. If the

Veteran can qualify for the payments, then fine. We don't want to have a foreclosure later.

Cheetah chasing time for some of you. This numbers 17 and 18 and named Lease/Option and Lease/Purchase.

Any transaction done incorrectly can be costly. A student of mine was getting her real estate license because her licensed husband had messed up big time on a Lease/Option – Way Number 17: A lease/option is not a sale. A lease/option is nothing more than a rental for a period with the option, at the end of the lease, of buying the property at the previously agreed price, locked in, and for you only for that time period. All one has to do is pick up the option (Opt) to buy the house and pay for it at that time. Only then is it a sale. Well, my student's husband had written up the lease/option papers and asked for $7,000. She said that after a year, the time period of the lease, they had trashed the house and wanted their $7,000 "deposit" back. The judge couldn't tell from the wording of the contract if the $7,000 was option money or was it lease deposit, and anytime the wording is misleading or incorrect, it goes against the one preparing it. So the judge ordered them to refund the "deposit." Wording should have included: $500 of this check is for the rental deposit and the remaining $6,500 shall be considered option money. Option money is NEVER refunded. It is payment to the owner for the locked in price, to them only, for a locked in time. If they opt to purchase, then the option money is part payment. In the above case it would have been more professional to ask for two checks, one for the lease deposit and another for the option money.

Many times the owner of a Lease/Option will sell the paperwork to someone else at a higher price, thus making a profit. (To keep it straight, the owner of the Lease/Option is not the owner of the property). He opts to purchase and immediately sells it at a double closing. This is totally legal and a way that many people earn their living. The lease/optionee is in total control. Of course if, at the end of the lease, he decides not to purchase, he opts out, he loses the option money. I won't use up way Number 19 on this selling of the paperwork, because, after all, it's just a Lease/Option.

A Lease/Purchase, Way: Number 18, is nothing more than a sales contract to purchase property with a delayed closing date. It is an actual sale, just awaiting the closing. Did you know that in America one can't die out of a sales contract? That's right. Neither the buyer nor the seller. It is sold! There is no cold foot law in purchasing property with the exception in some states. If one enters a purchase contract in Georgia for a Condominium type property, including Town Houses, and Time Share, one has seven days after all the paperwork to back out and be fully restored to his original position. I understand that Florida law allows ten days. The timeshare industry brought this about. People who had bought timeshare, later realizing what they had done, complained to their legislatures and got the law passed. The Cold Foot Law that you thought covered everything, only covers contracts that would place a lien on property already owned. If you contract to purchase a house and a flood takes it down the creek, you have purchased a lot. The same for fire, and tornadoes, etc. One needs special stipulations and correct wording in contracts—by professional real estate agents—to protect themselves.

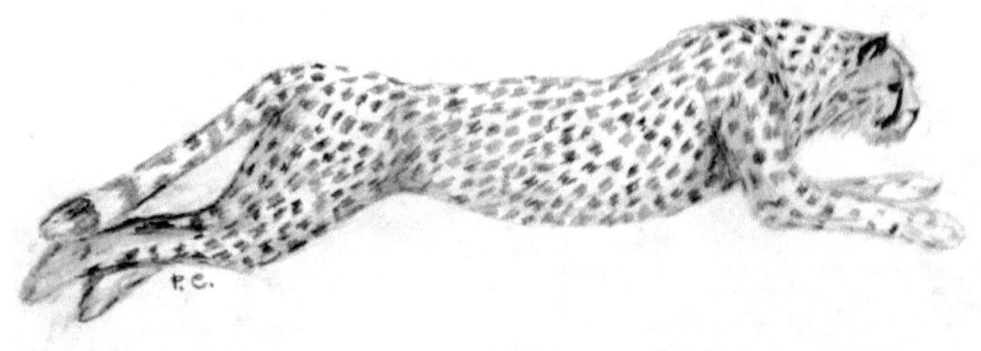

Back to Lease/Purchases. Two documents are required as in a lease/option. One of them will be an Exhibit attached to the other. In a Lease/Purchase the main document should be the sales contract. The exhibit will be the lease. When the delayed closing date arrives, the purchaser and seller go to closing. The main reason for this type of sale is generally to allow the buyer to accumulate enough down payment, etc. to qualify for the pending loan. Here's a Cheetah! Under special circumstances, say, the seller owns the house outright, and the price is right, in the sales contract, state that the $1,000 monthly rent will accrue to become earnest money—down payment. No. Hold on. I am not suggesting that the year's rent will be free. Let's say that you want to sell your house for $100,000. Don't forget to add for inflation in the year's time it is rented, say $3,000. Now the sales price seems to be $103,000. Not through. Make the agreed upon sales price $115,000—you add the $12,000 rent on to the price of the house. That way you have legitimately collected rent and spent it and, at the same time, have allowed the purchaser to accrue $12,000 earnest money, something that he would have had a very difficult time saving any other way. He qualifies for a 90% loan at the bank, the house will appraise for $115,000 and everyone is happy. This is NOT mortgage fraud because $15,000 is not unreasonable in a year's time and will probably fit into any neighborhood's wavy-line price range. You are not giving anybody anything here—you are renting and counting on inflation, the sales price is reasonable and will appraise. Otherwise, it could lead to Mortgage Fraud. The Wavy- Line Value in any neighborhood varies from $5,000 to $20,000, as you already know. Again, remember that I said that the price must be reasonable. You like that one? I do too.

Way Number 19—Cash. Need I say more? Yes. Just write out a check for the house. Don't forget to get title insurance, homeowners insurance, check all the zoning, restrictive covenants, all the usual things you would do on ALL, I REPEAT, ALL transactions, even if you are purchasing from your brother-in-law. ESPECIALLY IF YOU ARE PURCHASING FROM HIM!

Way Number 20 is "Seller takes back a second." Books call it a PMM—purchase money mortgage. We in the industry call it what it is—the seller takes back a second mortgage. In other words, this is a loan assumption and since the buyer didn't have enough cash to pay all of the seller's equity, the seller lends him the rest.

There is a very important caveat (warning) you need to be aware of. This loan assumption is like any other. The buyer begins paying off the seller's mortgage. If he fails to do so, then the seller gets foreclosed on and the buyer loses his home. Since it's the first mortgage that gets foreclosed on, any mortgage under that one (junior mortgage—second mortgage, etc. gets wiped out. So, when you allow your seller to take back a second mortgage, always have your lawyer include in the paperwork a "cross default clause." This clause allows the holder of the second mortgage, the seller, to foreclose first! That way he isn't wiped out. He steps in and satisfies the debt and takes back the house. Yes, we remember that ALL mortgages are now assumable—just include the limited power of attorney and record it.

Way Number 21 is perchance the weirdest way of all. If you are the buyer, simply sign a 100-year lease. Any lease for 100 years or more, at the end of the lease, the title to the property reverts to the tenant. 100-year leases. Therefore, the phenomenon of the ninety-nine-year leases. Nobody wants to sign more than 99 years, except tenants. One night in a real estate class a young lady said that she and her husband were dropping out of class. They had paid the tuition, the class was several weeks complete. They were both students also at Kennesaw University, trying to improve their lives, etc., and at the same time wanted a real estate license. The car they drove was the most gross Volkswagen bug you could imagine—but it ran. It happened that lawyers had contacted her from Texas. She happened to be the owner of the land under the Shell Oil Refinery in Texas and, now of age, it was time for a new land lease to be signed. Her uncle was no longer able to sign for her—the lawyers knew that. She wasn't even aware that she owned this land. They both returned to visit the class a couple weeks later. You should have seen what they drove up in—not the Volkswagen. She told the class that she had signed two ninety-nine-year leases with Shell Oil. Sadly they never finished the classes to get a real estate license! She also told the class that she got rid of the uncle. Maybe he had rat holed some funds. Wouldn't it have been nice if the uncle had said each month: "Hey, kids, here's a couple thousand dollars for you. One of these days you can look out for me also." One hundred- year leases—sign one if you are a tenant, don't if you are a seller.

Way Number 22 is Land contract. This simply means that the owner is going to be the bank and you simply pay him the agreed monthly payment, interest, etc. Caution: Have a real estate professional write the contract, or a lawyer. Have a closing with title insurance, all the regular precautions. Do not, repeat, do not purchase the house simply based on contract law! That is called a Land Contract. Frowned upon in all fifty states! It is illegal in some. After all, it is a way to purchase. It is called, as I have said Land contract. It is also called Contract for Deed. It is also named Installment Sales contract. What makes it so dangerous is that the seller retains title, just like when you buy a car. The dealership retains title. There is no foreclosure process. They just come pick up the car because you violated the terms of the contract. Say you purchase a house and agree to make 120 payments of $1,000—a $120,000 house. You make 119 payments and then are late on the very last payment. Since you violated the terms of the contract, the seller need only tell you to get out of his house. He has the title and the right to do so—contract law. Some states have enacted legislation that in the case of a seller's declaring the contract void, in these states the seller would have to reimburse the purchaser the monthly overage of economic rent, if any. Example: Normal rent (economic rent) in the area is $500 per month and the buyer is paying $600 per month on the land-contract, then the seller would reimburse him the $100 overage per month. In some states it is illegal to acknowledge (notarize) land-contracts for recordation. Caveat emptor—let the buyer beware. To over-simplify the above—in the case of the example I just gave, that would be considered a Title Theory State. The Mortgagee (Bank/Lender) has the right to repossession and rents. He already still had title. Other states are LienTheory States. That means that the mortgagor, the borrower/buyer holds title and the mortgagee (lender) has a lien on it. The property belongs entirely to the buyer, the rents thereof, profits, control, all belong to the owner, not the lender. The Land Contract is governed by contract law. There is no mortgage loan, no closing, no transfer of title, just contractual agreement. Either party that violates the contract, then the other party voids the contract. Usually, very little or no money is required as down payment—the purchaser begins making monthly payments. The seller usually refuses to have his signature notarized on the contract (It needs to be notarized in order to be recorded) to keep the buyer from recording the contract. If recorded, a "cloud" is then on the title. If the contract should be terminated with a cloud on the title, it is more difficult for the seller to sell to someone else until the title is cleared (the cloud removed).

At this time, in America, we (Congress that is) are voting for a bail-out of lending institutions. I am appalled at the word that in some states, people are allowed to try to buy houses they can't afford. That doesn't happen in Georgia. Georgia should be exempt from the "bail-out" expense. The Georgia Real Estate Commission, under the first leadership of Elmer Borgshatz and later Charles Clark, requires instructors to teach the basic ethical finance requirements for qualifying for home purchases. We teach real estate agents how to qualify their prospects. In Georgia you will not be shown properties out of your price range. We will not put you in our show car. If per chance you get a ding-a-ling agent who does not qualify you and shows you more property than you can afford, then the lending institution will squelch the sale. Georgia is the first state to pass a Residential Mortgage Fraud law. The penalties are harsh with jail time for anyone involved in mortgage fraud: Brokers/agents, lawyers, bankers, sellers, and buyers… to jail!

Basically, a person may qualify for a price range of two and one half times one's yearly salary. Then the bank sees to it that you don't spend more than one fourth of your monthly take-home. Then there are the expense ratios, debt service to income including utilities, food, etc. While the above is very conservative, they are the basics. Then there are more liberal entrees, but within reason. The main reason for foreclosures in Georgia is the Adjustable Rate Mortgage (ARM). A person buys a home for which he qualifies. If he doesn't plan and budget, soon his house payment is four hundred dollars more one month. Though he qualified at first, there is required some planning. A person gets a mortgage. He then listens to the ads from sleazy second mortgage companies "We will lend you 125% of your home value!" He starts refinancing. He is borrowing himself into foreclosure. A person who does this sort of thing should not be saved through bail-out. Not One Dime!

Having taught real estate courses and appraisal for thirty-five years, I know of no real estate agent involved in any of the above. I can't see it happen in Georgia. We are very strict on ourselves.

Way Number 23 is to buy it from the REO (Real Estate Owned) department at the bank. They have foreclosed upon the loan and now have title and may sell the house to any qualified buyer that they choose. Here, let me tell you what I learned from John Adams radio program. Mr. Adams has found out that if you make an early bid on a just-foreclosed house, the committee (bank committee), who is in charge of unloading this unwanted real estate, will generally turn down the first bid, especially if it comes in too early, say, the first week after foreclosure (early in the week). Thinking that this piece of real estate is real hot, the committee will turn down offers, hoping to get more and better offers on this hot one. What Mr. Adams does, and he says it works, he has already done the research and picked out the house under foreclosure. He offers the bank 75% of their asking price. It is turned down. Three weeks later he halves his offer and says that they jump on it! That means picking up a property at 37.5% of its value! You like that one? There has to be a cheetah in there somewhere. Get up the courage and go for it! Generally, the banks want cash for the REO's. You might prearrange credit, or with very good credit and references, be able to finance a REO at that bank. Banks are there to make a profit and will work with you if you just ask. Be ready to negotiate.

Here's a banking tip that I'll call Way Number 24. It's called Single Payment note and can be very useful if you buy at an auction which I will combine here into just one way. At an auction, they want ten percent down and the balance in twenty-four hours. My wife and I bid at an auction and I found myself the highest bidder. I went to our bank for the 90% balance, which we had in a CD. Not knowing bank jargon, I thought that I wanted an Interest Only loan without making payments and then pay them back in one year, interest and principle. I was informed that that was called a Single Payment Loan. "That's what I want," I said. It was my own money I was borrowing. She said "You can't do thayette." "Why not?" I replied. "I'll have to talk to my supervisor," she said. Directly, two girls returned, one being the supervisor who told me "You can't do thayette." So, I left and went to the same bank—different branch and asked the loan officer for a one-year single payment note that I would borrow out of our CD. She said that her one-year portfolio was full, but that she could lend me the note on a two-year term—no payments for two years! Results: I was allowed to borrow the sufficient amount, but not all, the money in the CD at 9% interest, all to be paid back in two years. Meanwhile, the entire original CD note would continue to accrue interest at 7%. Wow! Meaning I received a loan of my own money at the real rate of 2%! Almost a cheetah! Do you agree? I'm sure that many of you already knew that one. Banks enjoy negotiating. They make loans for a profit.

Another tip: If you happen to be one of those people who are transferred every four or five years, why apply for a 30-year mortgage. You aren't going to pay much principle before being transferred again, so ask for a Straight Note. This one is important in real estate financing and strategy. This one is interest only, monthly, just like house payments, and then one day, when the note is due, you go in and pay it all off. Make sure there is no Prepayment-Penalty, but that you have Prepayment Privilege rights. We also call that an "Or More" loan: You are supposed to pay $800 per month "or more." Hence, every dime you spend each month on house payments will be tax deductible under our present laws. Your aim is not to pay off the house in thirty years anyway. You sell the house when the transfer comes up, pay it off, move on to Texas—or wherever, and get another Straight Note in the new location. Some of us in real estate get referrals from the happy people we introduced to this plan. You are looking out for the needs and benefits of your buyers without jeopardizing the sellers.

Another banking tip for fellow real estate agents: Always, when you accompany your people to the bank for their loan application, take them to the bank president's office, always. Introduce them. She will take them to her loan officer while you go for coffee. Get yourself an alphabetized address book to keep a record of each loan, name, address, amount of the loan on the page for each bank, mortgage company you deal with. Upon leaving the bank, total up this present loan with the above and you will have a running total for each bank. One day, there will be a money shortage. They are cyclical. When that happens, banks are only lending to their best customers—GE—Coca Cola—General Motors, etc., not customers of Joe Real Estate. At this time, after the bank president has introduced your buyers to her loan officer, say this, "By the way, let me show you my little record of the business I bring to your bank." She will say how wonderful you are and "can I get you some coffee?" You see, when there is a monetary crunch, the banks don't offer coffee as usual. At this point, remind her that you qualify your buyers for her bank, Fannie Mae, etc. and that you realize there is a money crunch, but that you need her help this time—waving your little book at her. She is on the loan committee and will see that your people, this time, get the loan that they qualify for and deserve. I call that one the Clout Loan and I learned that at a real estate seminar years ago. It works. This is a tool for real estate agents to use when a possible loan looks to be very close to borderline, but is deemed to be deserving. Since it is also a manner (enticement), way to secure a loan and get the job done, I have decided to use it as Way 25, if you will.

One more banking tip that I will call Way Number 26. Banks versus Banks is the name of this number twenty-six, just to be successful at loan application. My wife, Pilar, sold a house to a lady back when it was sometimes difficult for ladies, especially single ladies, to get a loan. I barged in on this sale and found out where she banked. Her bank didn't make home loans. I took her there anyway. I introduced her to the president and said that she, their depositor, was here for a home loan! The president informed us that they didn't make home loans to whom I said, "Well she banks here and here we are. Can you recommend or do anything?" He said "Let me make a phone call." He called Cobb Federal and talked to Al Hallman, President, and said that he was sending James Clinkscales and Ms Buyer up there for a home loan. When we arrived, Al took her over to the loan department and said "Fix her up with a home loan." Here you have one bank president asking another bank president for something. It worked. I must add here that it didn't hurt that Al Hallman was president of the board of trustees one year during my four-year term as Headmaster of Joseph T. Walker School in Marietta. All of your bank contacts can pay off sooner or later.

These next two ways to buy a house, Ways Numbers 27 and 28, are called SAM (Shared Appreciation Mortgages). There are basically two ways because one of them involves the bank. The other is private: You don't have enough money for the down payment, or your income isn't sufficient to make the monthly payments. The lender will put up all or part of the down payment, or he can offer you a below-market rate or even pay a portion of the monthly payments. The lender and you are joint partners. You both set an agreed upon date in writing. At that time you either sell the house or refinance it. At this date the lender gets his share up to that time. Within three, five or ten years that you agreed upon, you beg, steal, borrow, refinance the home. May I say that it's better to get half of a house than all of none. You then can use your one half as down payment on your own entire house. It's a great way to begin and banks love it. Remember, they are in the business of making money. The above works best in times of "good" inflation. We like that in real estate.

Your co-partner may be a friend, relative, boss. Whoever that person is will share the appreciation—the sharee (no, not French). Many times the lender will want a long term. This is to his advantage unless he needs his cash in a shorter time period. Remember that the house is appreciating (increasing in value) daily and last year's appreciation and yesterday's is also appreciating. If the end of the term happens to be a "bad" time to borrow, refinance, sell, or there could be personal reasons, you may offer the lender another 2, 3, 4, 5% of the equity at a later date. Just draw up new papers giving him this larger share. You are both benefiting. Keep in mind, or put it there if it weren't there already, that briefly, the 1st and 2nd mortgages must not exceed 80% of the appraised value or sale price, whichever is lower.

Way Number 29 I will call UP HIS APPRECIATION, or PAY MORE THAN IT IS WORTH. Be aware that many houses are under-priced, many or well-priced and many are over-priced. No house is really over-priced, the timing is just off. It is just that the right buyer for it was born the same day it was priced—they both have to age somewhat. You really need and want a house (everybody needs and wants a house), but you don't have the cash on hand, or you have offered his price but he won't help with the financing, here's an excellent way to entice him to help finance. Appreciation is altered by adjusting the sales price. You are trying to buy a $150,000 house. In one year using 10% appreciation, the house will be worth $165,000. I realized that I used a very high inflation rate, but you get the point. Offer to buy it at that price. In two years it will be worth $181,500. Offer him that! All you are doing is giving up two years of equity at 10%, and you are now among the Homeowners of America Club! If he will finance for you but wants an exorbitant interest rate, offer him more price to lower those payments. If he wants to amortize the loan over 2 – 5 years, making your payments uncomfortable, offer him more price for 10 – 15 years. Horse-trade with him. You both want the same thing. He wants out, you in. Everybody wins. I could have entitled this one "More than they are asking," instead of "More than it's worth," because something is worth what someone is willing to take or pay for it. It was worth-it to you to pay more.

Technical time: If you are not interested, just skip this section. I want to explain "Interest rate." It is a way to purchase a house, but I will not waste a number on it. It is simply a finance method. We call it, in the industry, a pledged account mortgage (PAM), and/or a Buy Down. The pledged account mortgages and the buy-downs have changed in meaning and have interchanges so much that everything is now being called a buy-down. It becomes important to know just what is being bought-down. First, let's define the terms. There is the NOTE RATE, the INTEREST RATE, the PAYMENT RATE, and the ANNUAL PERCENTAGE RATE (APR). They mean different things to different people. The note rate, a banker's term (now it's our term), means the interest rate that is stated on the note itself for the duration of the term-fixed rate of 15% for 30 years, or 15% during this 3-month adjusted (ARM) period. The note rate is the rate from which you buy down. If you call the bank and ask what the interest rate is, they may quote you 13% which may be the bought-down (subsidized) rate. Then ask them if that is the note rate. It may be different. At least now you are talking the same language. To the general public, the interest rate is what they signed up for and agreed to pay each month, the payment rate. Among the real estate industry (bankers and brokers) there is still some confusion with the term "interest rate." The banker maybe quoting interest rate-the bought-down rate, and the broker is thinking note rate but using the term "interest rate." To the general public everything is interest rate. It is really quite simple: take the starting point-note rate. You can buy it down temporarily and it is known as a subsidy or pledged account mortgage (PAM), and you can buy it (note rate) down permanently and it is known as buying down the note rate (interest rate). Both transactions are now known as buy-downs.

Here is how to buy-down one percent of interest. There are, in theory, eight (8) discount points contained in each percentage of interest. Say, the bank offers you a loan for six (6) percent interest. You think that six percent is too high to pay for 30 years. You would like a five percent mortgage. You can buy the interest down to five percent! Say that your loan is to be $100,000 at six percent. To get rid of one percent interest, you need to pay the bank up front the one percent at closing. To do this (remember that there are eight discount points in each one percent of interest) simply pay the bank 8% of the mortgage up front ($100,000 times 8%), or $8,000 and you have bought the mortgage rate down to five! To buy one half percent down, you would pay $100,000 times four percent ($4000). Duh! Remember that it takes (present market) eight points (discount) to equal one percent times the mortgage. During the Carter years, there were six discount points contained in one percent of interest! You can count on eight, presently. This could change for the worse. Tomorrow, November 4, Obama may become president! A little bit of history there. Remember, this is my book. Just keeping things in perspective.

The Annual Percentage Rate (APR) is neither the note rate nor the payment rate. In July, 1996, a federal law became effective known as Truth-In-Lending and was implemented by Regulation Z of the Federal Reserve Board. It is concerned with the following. If real estate credit is offered that involves a finance charge, or by agreement, is payable in more than four installments (not for business purposes unless agriculture), then there must be disclosure of the relationship of the total finance charge with the amount to be financed. So, the buyer goes to closing and sees 15% interest on the papers and he was told and knows that he signed up for 14%, he hits the ceiling! Calm down! Your payments are based on simple interest of 14%, just as you signed up for. The 15% simply means that the government wants you to be aware that all of the finance charges and part of the closing costs are added to show the true yield (profit) to the lender. The prepaid finance charges most often required by lenders in real estate transactions and which necessarily are included in the Annual Percentage Rate, are (but not limited to): prepaid interest, discount points, origination fee, mortgage insurance, lender's commitment fee, warehouse fee, and appraisal, investigation and credit report.

Now Way Number 30. And, yes it is the PAM (Pledged Account Mortgage). In a high-interest market, people who have good jobs and good credit and who would normally be able to buy a house, sometimes find that they can't afford the monthly payments quoted them. In order to get them into a house, the builder, developer, seller, will place with the lender sufficient funds to subsidize the buyer's monthly mortgage payments. Depending on the investor, a seller may pledge up to 3% for up to five years. This money is paid up front. The seller receives no interest (his interest is subsidizing the buyers' house payments) this only benefit is that he was able to sell the house. The borrower must qualify for the bought-down payments. When the subsidy runs out, the purchaser should anticipate paying the original (before the buy-down) payments (note rate payments). Of course, by now (three years) he has received raises enough to qualify in his salary. The seller, investor, developer, at the end of the three years, receive their money back. Anyone can pay the subsidy, the seller, the buyer, the preacher. Most lenders allow pledged accounts from three to five years. This is because that is the maximum allowed by Fannie Mae, the one who buys the mortgages from the banks. Caveat! The buyer should be told, made aware, shown, waked up, pointed-out to, that the interest rate or payment rate in this case is NOT the note rate (make him read this book), and that his payments will revert back to the note rate payments. He can then make plans and budget or/and sell or refinance when the time comes. So, be very careful when you see in the advertisement of flyer 11% interest! The whole key is communication and understanding. It has been said that nothing is quite so clear as one's own perception of something!

Way Number 31 is the Straight Note or Straight Term Mortgage that I mentioned in the introduction. Remember, interest only during the term and then when the note is finally due, you pay off the entire loan at that time. When our grandparents used to purchase houses/farms, this was the only game in town except paying cash. This mortgage allows you to buy a house now and gives you time to finance it later. You also get to deduct all of your monthly payments because they are interest only. Straight term means that the loan isn't amortized and is usually for a short term, 3– 5 years, and is renewable at the end of said term. Interest payments are made periodically but no principal payments. This is especially good for people who are transferred on a regular basis from town to town. Why should they amortize a loan when they don't expect to live there more than three or four years? This way, all the monthly payments (interest) is tax deductible under our present IRS laws—very good for some people. This loan differs from the Balloon note in that the principal in the balloon note is usually amortized. This loan is attractive to the seller if he doesn't need/want his money now and who may be in a better tax position later. For the purchaser, it is good if he can vision a sale prior to the end of the term. Again, make sure that there is no pre-payment penalty, or that you have an "Or More" clause in the loan papers. Here I must mention PREPAYMENT PRIVILEGE, called the "Or More" clause. Without this clause, you have no right to pay the loan off until the end of the term. This holds true in any loans with definite exceptions for FHA and VA loans. If no such right exists, you have an open mortgage. The seller cannot be forced to accept prepayment on a closed mortgage even if the purchaser defaults on purpose to trigger the acceleration clause. The courts have ruled that such clauses are for the seller/creditor's benefit and he may or may not choose to enforce the acceleration clause. If your papers contain such words as "or more" (monthly installments of $852 or more) or "not less than" (monthly payments of not less than $852), then you have an open mortgage. The wording may spell it out: "purchaser may pre-pay the entire balance or installments thereof."

Earlier I mentioned the 1099 Shortfall, where a bank forgives the balance you owe when they foreclose and receive less than the mortgage due at the foreclosure sale. Say you owe $200,000. At the foreclosure sale the house only brings $175,000. The bank usually forgives you the "overage." Well, the IRS, bless their hearts, charges you tax on the "forgiven" debt of $25,000, calling it income. Here's how you may avoid that tax burden. It is called a "Short Sale." Take the same set of circumstances. Say you owe the $200,000. Rather than let the bank foreclose on it, you sell it for $175,000, with the bank's permission. The bank pardons the $25,000. Since you sold the house, not taking a second mortgage, or lien, there is no tax penalty (Whoever thought that one up!). Had they foreclosed—tax penalty or charge. I won't use up a Way to Buy a House on that one, but it is a Way to Sell sometimes and in some markets. Good luck! Let's get rid of IRS. There are movements about. Join one.

It's time to get creative. We simply call it creative financing. During the hard times during Jimmy Carter, there was no money—the interest rate got up to 21%, so we (not I, but I copied it all down.) invented ways to finance homes. Remember the loan assumptions? Seller takes back a second mortgage? How do you talk a seller into doing so—lending the buyer the money? I suggest you also read *Swim With The Sharks Without Being Eaten Alive,* by Harvey Mackay, wherein he wants all his sales people to know sixty-one things about the customer. They sell envelopes! How complicated a product! And, to know sixty-one things about buyers, you really know their likes, dislikes, needs, etc. In real estate, if a salesperson knows that many things about his people, then he can put together a sale, keeping in mind their needs. I took Mr. Mackay's list and shortened it to about fifth or so. There are things I don't want to know. I will call this next way to buy, Way Number 32, "Rule of 72." The rule of 72 is simply that if you divide into 72 the interest rate, the results will be how many years it would take that investment to double if you left interest and principle at compounded interest. Example: 6% interest, and you have a savings of $30,000. Six goes into seventy-two twelve times. In other words, if you left the $30,000 in the account for twelve years compounding, at the end you would have $60,000—Rule of 72. You know that your seller is going to put the money from the sale of the house into the bank drawing a whopping 2% interest. Two goes into 72 thirty-six times. In thirty-six years he will double his money. You instruct him: "Mr. Seller, I can get your money doubled, not in thirty-six years, but in six." you have his interest. At 12% interest that the buyer is able and willing to pay, you work your deal and both buyer and seller are happy. The buyer's credit wasn't exactly perfect (that record collection he ordered as a teenager, etc. He saves high loan costs, closing costs, etc. Remember to include the cross-default clause, etc., for the seller's protection. Again, this clause allows the seller to foreclose first in case the buyer defaults on the first mortgage, etc.

More creative financing: When sellers take back a second mortgage, the seller then has a negotiable note with which he can deal, sell, borrow against, or just hold on to it till it is paid. If he takes that note to the bank, or the mortgage company on the corner-Lendum and Watchum Squirm Mortgage, they may give him fifty cents on the dollar. The seller needed funds after all. If the seller needed future funds, the bank would want more collateral—they already have his note—"What else do you have to use as collateral?" Let's do it this way, and I'll use up Way Number 33—Partial Sale. Simply take the same note to the bank and work out the following: Here's my note. I need this amount of money. My buyer, instead of paying me, will be paying directly to you until this loan from you to me is paid off. Then you return to me the note and he will pay to me. That way the seller isn't making monthly payments to the bank on the loan—Partial sale.

Creative financing contd. Instead of giving the seller a note for the, say, $30,000, give the seller three notes! This works beautifully in Commercial Real Estate deals. He gets a $10,000 2nd mortgage at two percent interest, a $10,000 3rd mortgage at four percent interest, and a 4th mortgage of $10,000 at six percent interest. The buyer is still paying a blend of twelve percent, he is happy. Now the seller, your client, has three negotiable documents to play with instead of the just one. Although that is just another way of working a loan, I'm going to use up Way Number 34 on it—Seller Excitement Loan.

Continuing the creative financing, let's use up Way Number 35—Rule of 78. This is basically, and I will get argument on this, a way to preclude pre-payment. The seller wants the loan to be paid out with all the interest. I understand that the Jim Walter Homes company sells their homes in this manner. My daughter bought one of their homes on a loan assumption from a seller. At closing the loan was $28,000. If the loan had been paid off, the total was $59,000, all the interest accrued that the company would have received had the loan reached maturity. Why would anyone use this method? Many people don't need the immediate money from a sale—IRS! So, by using the Rule of 78, a precluding of pre-payment. Works for a lot of people. You are supposed to find out their needs, remember? I sold my parents' house for them in that manner. They didn't need the sale money to live on. Their pensions, annuities, etc, were enough with the "monthly payments," to live on very comfortably, avoiding the big tax consequences of receiving a lump sum at closing—as opposed to what we call Pre-Payment Privilege Clause, or also, the "Or More" clause, allowing one to pay the, say $792 per month, or more.

This Way Number 36, I call the Transfer Account Loan. It is similar to the PAM (Pledged Account Mortgage), where the builder, seller, puts up an amount drawing interest in order to subsidize the buyer's payments. That we did during the Jimmy Carter years. A buyer signs up to buy a house with ten percent interest. By the time closing came around, the interest was sixteen percent. He no longer qualified for the loan. Here we are going to talk to the bank in banker's language. Buyers love to do banking business where they have established a certain rapport. This is normal and can be a big plus as to whether they get a house loan or not. Talk the seller into transferring his banking business to your bank as an inducement for the bank to give you that loan. When it comes down to making a sale (means money in their pocket) or not, sellers will gladly establish new banking contacts. Business is business. They were probably looking for an excuse to transfer anyway. Different banks (where you've just transferred) always treat one so wonderfully! If the seller and purchaser already do business at the same bank, it wouldn't hurt to let the banker know (from the seller) just how important it is for him to make that sale. This is called clout —clout has been defined as flexing one's muscles, or throwing one's weight around. The amount of weight throwable in this case depends on the size of his bank account. Duh!

You now know about the Pledged Account Mortgage and the Transfer Account Loan, so I want to talk now about the Buydown. You should know that in today's market, one percent of interest over thirty years theoretically equals eight (8) discount points. And, you should know that to convert a discount point into dollars, you simply multiply that point (percent) times the loan: $100,000 loan times one discount point equals $1,000. That was one discount point, equaling $1,000. Say that you do not want a nine percent loan, but that you want an eight percent loan. That's easy. Just buy down the interest rate. Remember that there are eight discount points in one percent of interest. $100,000 loan at nine percent interest. Pay the bank the eight discount points contained in one percent of interest. $100,000 times eight percent. That's $8,000! You have just bought the interest down to the eight percent interest that you wanted. You didn't think that the bank would forgive one percent, did you? They get the money (interest equivalent) up front, that's all. During the Carter years, I have seen builders buy down the interest rate so that the buyer could afford to buy their houses. The builder took a beating, but he was able to move inventory rather than go into foreclosure himself—Buy-downs—Way Number 37. I always wondered if, say, you had a ten percent loan offered you, could you buy down the entire interest rate? For a $100,000 loan at ten percent, could you give them the $80,000 (eight discount points times ten) and walk away with a no interest loan? Interesting thought. You would pay principal only for the thirty years.

Here's Way Number 38 to buy (sell) a house: I call it the Bank Stock Purchase Loan: There are sellers who really don't have immediate need of the funds they receive in the sale of their real property (Remember the Rule of 72?), A very good inducement for the bank to make their purchaser a loan is for the seller to purchase bank stock. Now, we are talking the banker's language. Enough stock purchased by your seller, makes the banker his employee. I liked that one too. No Cheetah, though.

Though there are many more Ways to come, they have been getting a little lame lately, for me, anyway. You already have thirty-eight ways to buy a house, and some of you are probably thinking, wow, if the opportunity ever arises, I can use one or more of these ways to swing into action. If a Cheetah happens by, I'll just grab his tail! I'm prepared! Well, let me tell you this: If you want a better life, you are a loser! Yeah, a big fat loser! Let's start over: If you <u>expect</u> a better life, then you are a winner. There's a vast difference in wanting and expecting. I call it: DOING THAT THING! Ease over into that left lane where the action is, where the passing goes on, and where you aren't stuck behind a slowpoke. If you are a lineman on the football team—you are big and strong, in shape (the reason you are there), don't just wait for a Cheetah to come by, CAUSE A FUMBLE, RECOVER ONE, MAKE SOMETHING HAPPEN! You are in the backfield, one of the best. You don't just wait for something to happen, you cause it. If a ball comes your way, a Cheetah, you will catch it. You were supposed to write down last night that you were going to CAUSE a fumble, you were going to INTERCEPT A PASS. DO THAT THING! You aren't going to succeed waiting for an opportunity. YOU WERE SUPPOSED TO CAUSE ONE.

One of my favorite Cheetah catchers, and I have talked about her to all my classes—she won't mind—is Jeanne Roberts, a consummate professional, honest, ethical, a great lady! Once upon a time, when she had been in real estate for about a year, it wasn't happening for her. She decided to get out of real estate. She had a meeting of the minds with her husband and decided to give it one more year. However!!! This next year was going to be different! With no more money coming in, she decided to hire a secretary! A secretary to do the $5 per hour work, leaving her free every day to do the hundreds of dollars per hour work. Guess what! She became the number one agent in Coldwell Banker that year, surpassing all the other super agents with name recognition. She moved over into the left lane. She can't be beat. She did THAT THING! She doesn't wait for a Cheetah to come by. She goes looking for him! Of course, there are thousands of real estate agents, and people in all other walks of life, ready and prepared. But, they are riding along in the right lane, always ready, but not making it happen. So sad!

Another Cheetah catcher that I'd like to tell you about is a young man that I was fortunate enough to have in one of my continuing education classes. I don't have his name, but he will recognize himself. He drives an ambulance for a living (pass time), but sells more real estate than anyone else in his company. He loves driving that ambulance. One should do what he loves. Here is his secret: Every morning, before getting into his ambulance, he places ten business cards in his shirt pocket. He does not return home until he has given out all ten cards to ten different people. They become customers, etc. Ten business cards!

Here, let me tell you how to give away cards. You always offer the card to someone upside down saying: "Put this into your active file." They will immediately turn it over and say "Oh, you are in real estate" (whatever your business). You say, "Do you need my help, or do you know anyone who does?" Remember, you have just purchased a pack of gum from him. People tend to want to do business with anyone who has just given him business. They will invariably say "Why, my aunt is going to sell her house." You are writing down her name on another card. "You aren't going to call her are you?" "Sure am, and I'll tell her you said hello." There's a Cheetah in there somewhere.

Here's an idea for you bold (You're going after Cheetahs, aren't you?). My wife and I used to purchase season tickets for the Falcons. Sitting up behind the end zone one day someone threw fliers out into the stadium. They were coordinated. Several people threw fliers out at just the same time from the upper deck and they floated down among the throng. Well, I didn't get one! I had to climb over a very dangerous fencing to get one. They were selling religion, I already had some, so I threw it back. The next week, however, I took a box of my business cards to the game. It wasn't coordinated—just I. My wife knew where I was because I would go to one exit and throw a handful of my cards out. Then I would run to the next exit and do the same. Guess what. I got calls! Some people called just to see who that nut was who was throwing out his cards. One in particular said that he and his wife had been talking that morning about the possibility of selling their house and that they wanted an "aggressive" agent, did I work Cobb County? Definite Cheetah there.

One more card story? A new agent of mine came into the office one morning and was giving everyone in the office her new business card. An older gentleman, agent, was sitting back with his feet on the desk, told her "Don't give me one of those. Cards don't work! I still have the first five hundred cards that I ever bought. They don't work. I should have fired him. He doesn't work! Remember, upside down—and the speech.

Dear Diary, it's January 8, 2009 and everything in my life is changed! I was retired the last month of 2008 and I no longer have an audience as I used to have to whom to tell my stories and to have fun with people. As they say about teachers, we finally lose our class. Headmasters (I used to be one) lose their faculties. And not to forget lawyers, they lose their appeal, and doctors lose their patients. Well, since I no longer will be teaching, I am putting my favorite stories into this book. Therefore, this book is also changed. I have already told you about two Cheetah catchers and there are a couple more on the way. Can you imagine, if someone of you, Gentle Readers, as Miss Manners, columnist, calls you, would emulate even one of these Cheetah catchers, you would become successful? What if you copied each of them? We would be reading about you pretty soon! I know, some of you are already successful, or don't need to become successful and only bought this book to get the Ways To Buy A House. You don't even know where point Z is (you didn't do the little exercise at the front of this book), and never will find out where you are going, although you might eventually, and luckily, get there. I still love you for buying this book and yes, there are many, many more Ways coming up.

First, here is another Cheetah catcher. David Vaughn was one of my students. After becoming licensed he came and told me one day of his plan. Every night he was going to call fifty people, if it took that many, or until he could get an appointment. I thought that that was a lot of calls and asked him if he was going to use the phone book. He said no, that he was going to call people on streets that he would pick out, streets that he wanted to do business on, and call those people living there. To do this in Atlanta, we have a service called the Haines Directory, a huge book that each office has and most of us get it personally for our particular area. Part of this book, which we rent every year, and swap it in every Fall, has all the listed phone numbers that you can look up numerically. It tells the name of the persons owning that phone, their mailing address, etc.

Imagine what a convenience! If you call a FSBO (For Sale By Owner), who, of course, didn't include his name in his newspaper ad, and call him by name, he is impressed, thinking that you know him. That turns a cold call into a warm knock! The other half of this Haines Directory contains all the streets by name. You look up, for example, Peach Street. There are many Peach Streets in Atlanta, but you look for the one in Cobb County and find out who lives on that street, the supposed income of that street, their address, and their phone number. Slick! Slick is good. Not Slickee. Slickee is the crook. Well, David looked up fifty names on his special streets and I got a call from him that first night. I'm not even his broker. He called at eleven thirty, the time that Johnny Carson came on with his monologue. I always watched the monologue, then went along to bed. The phone rang just as Ed McMahon said "Heeeere's Johnny!" David told me that he only had to call nine people to get that first appointment. The next night, sure enough, after "Heeeere's Johnny," the phone rang. Wow, it only took six calls to get the appointment. The next night it was eight calls. Even I was extremely excited by now, and no longer minded missing Johnny's monologue. David found out that from six to nine calls was all it took to get an appointment! He turned those appointments into listings and sales. He led his company!

What did David tell those people? I don't know, but it probably went like this: This is what I would say. "Hello, my name is James Clinkscales and I am a real estate agent. The reason for my call is this. I was riding down Peach Street today and noticed your house and was wondering if you would like a copy of the market analysis that I am doing on your street next Wednesday. It will give you an idea of what your house is presently worth. It's free and I can drop it off to you, say, would four-ten or four-twenty be most convenient?" Notice, Gentle Reader, that I didn't say "Would four or five be more convenient. That sounds like an hour with a salesman!

How many times have people told me "Why, Mr. Clinkscales, you are a God-send! Why, just this morning, my husband and I were discussing and wondering how much our house would bring. Yes, four-twenty this Wednesday would be wonderful. See you then. Thank you for calling." They blamed my call on God! Call fifty people every night. For those of you who are worrying, no, this is not telemarketing! Telemarketing is done by a machine, calling thousands of calls per hour. They will call and hang up on you, only wanting to know if a human answered on Tuesday at six-fifteen p.m. They then sell that info to a human who calls you the next Tuesday, at six-fifteen, to try to sell you something. If your phone is always ringing and no one is there, it is a machine. I learned this from Andy Rooney. Have your finger ready and when there is no one there, hit the pound button as fast as you can about seven times. This confuses the machine and erases your name and number from its data bank. My wife and I have virtually eliminated all those obnoxious calls and it only took a couple months, using Andy Rooney's suggestion. Thanks, Andy!

I will be brief on this next Cheetah catcher. This person probably has the best work-ethic that I have ever heard about. This person, Monday through Friday, from one to one-thirty p.m., calls ten FSBOS (For Sale By Owners). Their numbers are in the newspaper, and they are waiting for someone to call. This person has unbelievable success. You have noticed that each of the previous "Cheetah Catchers" has a particular Thing that they do. They aren't sitting around hoping for a good day. They are doing something while the rest of us are doing our best! One of my former students, Michael Selman, calls me on occasion—I look forward for his calls, told me one day "Coach, do you know when it is that one has a slump in real estate? It's when you don't do nothing!" What a profound statement! Michael is now a broker and owns his own company in Cartersville, Ga. and is one of the most successful businessmen in that town. You can see why! Go get 'em Michael!

Back to the Ways: Number 39. I call this Way the Company Interest-Free Loan. Your company can give you a no-interest loan to buy a house. The interest you save per year is the same as a raise. You have to report it, but you can claim an equal, offsetting interest deduction. You don't owe the tax. Your company benefits by keeping you happy, they claim a deduction for the income that they could have charged as interest. Note: you need professional advice on this one because the company gets a mortgage, you promise to keep working there, or if you leave, pay off the balance. Instead of investing the money and paying tax on the income, they get a deduction on what they could have charged you in interest.

That's about all I care to tell you, but it is worth looking into. Check out the New Tax Reform Act, circa 1987.

Number 40. This is called a Swing Loan or a Bridge Loan way to buy a house. When someone is transferred to a new location, there's always the anxious period between selling the present home in the old location and buying a new home at the new one. You need the funds from the present to buy the new. Several years ago, Trust Company Bank of Atlanta announced an Executive Swing loan Program to assist transferred executives of national and regional companies such interim financing. Perchance your bank in your town does or will do the same. There were salary minimums, at least two years seniority, you had to bank there, and the standard credit criteria, etc. The bank would loan up to the equity balance in the former home, less sales commissions, closing costs, up to a certain maximum—then $7500. It would be a six-month loan. If the former house had not sold by then, then the bank would take a second mortgage on the new home with the assurance of the proceeds of the home being sold as security. Many times a person from the North is transferred to the South and the northern home is under snow! Can't really sell it till they can find it in the Spring thaw—makes sense. Check with your bank.

Number 41. I call this next Way the Neal Boortz Savings Plan. There is someone out there who will use this idea to purchase a house. How many times have you heard people say "I can't save money!" They are wrong. Every one of us can save money, for a down payment, for Christmas shopping, for that emergency, for almost anything. Years ago, and he has probably forgotten this, Neal Boortz, conservative, syndicated, radio talk show host told us of his method of spending cash while Christmas shopping instead of using credit cards, and it works! That next year, my wife and I went through the Town Center Mall with wads of one-dollar bills. The idea is to save dollar bills. At the end of each day, put any and all one-dollar bills in a safe place for keeping. Just the one-dollar bills. They begin to accumulate. It is even addictive. You find yourself breaking a five so as not to spend that one-dollar bill. After breaking the five, you have other one-dollar bills to put away later. Over the year, you have accumulated enough to spend cash at Christmas.

Now, the only one-dollar bills that I spend are on the Georgia Lotto, my retirement plan! Of course, and it goes without saying (I'm going to say it), put all your change in a wine jug at the end of the day also. Change accumulates! Drink the wine first! I ought to tell you that I have quit drinking. I don't drink any more. No, now I use a funnel! After a while you will need to roll up the change coins in those coin rolls you get free from the bank: 40 quarters—ten dollars, two dollar rolls for nickels, five dollar dimes, and 50 cents for pennies. You take those rolls to the bank and guess what you exchange them for? Ta dah! Yes, one-dollar bills to put in the safe place! A word of caution, a caveat (watch out): Those coin tubes are supposed to hold the exact above sums. The penny tubes no longer work! They are making pennies thinner than they used to so that a penny tube holds fifty-two pennies! You must count them out. Yeah. I found out the hard way one day. I had been giving the bank fifty-two cents! Careful. All the other tubes seem to still work. Now, go out there and save up enough for that down payment. I'd love to hear from you when it works, o.k.?

Way number 42 is the Wrap-around Mortgage. When the interest rate got so high that no one could afford to buy a house, we began to use creative financing (this book is loaded with it) to get people into housing. If a mortgage happened to be assumable, we of course did that, but what a shame to let go of a very attractive interest of, say, six percent. Of course one wouldn't pay off the six percent mortgage so that the bank could take that money and lend it back out at eighteen percent. Loan assumptions were ok but the seller didn't really enjoy or get in on the act and still had to take back a second mortgage to get rid of the house! Hence the wrap-around mortgage.

The seller's first mortgage of $30,000 is at six percent interest. He has a high equity of $60,000. Sales price is $100,000. The buyer only has ten thousand dollars to give the seller. That leaves $50,000 to come up with. We take the $30,000 loan and add it to the missing $50,000 making $80,000. The seller takes back a second mortgage of $80,000 at twelve percent interest. The going rate is, say, sixteen percent, whatever. The seller continues to pay his first mortgage of six percent each month until maturity, with the money coming in on the $80,000 second mortgage. He is now making six percent profit on his first mortgage and twelve percent on $50,000. He is happy. The buyer is happy, he couldn't afford sixteen percent. There were no origination fees, high closing costs, etc., just normal attorney fees for doing the transaction. There are many caveats to be aware of to protect the buyer, making sure that the seller continues to pay off the first mortgage. There are also caveats to protect the seller. I won't go into all the caveats here. One needs to consult the closing attorney who knows how to protect all parties. This one is incorporating a loan assumption along with the seller's taking back a second mortgage. Don't forget to do the limited power of attorney, etc. My personal input into the wrap-around is this. Ideally, the buyer would pay his monthly payment to an account at the bank, who would then from their funds pay the first mortgage, then send to all, including the real estate agent, notice that it had been paid. The balance each month would, of course, go to the seller.

Number 43 is just more of the same. It is called the Magic Wrap. Back when the wrap-around mortgage was having its heyday, the banks were upset because we were not repaying the mortgages upon resale of the house. Fannie Mae was extremely upset because they weren't getting their money also (remember the rule of 72?). They were used to receiving all their money in six or seven years. That is when Fannie Mae required us (Georgia) to insert paragraph 17 in all our mortgages, or they wouldn't purchase Georgia mortgages. We capitulated immediately, of course. Back to the Magic Wrap. Since most mortgages back then were assumable and there wasn't a thing the bank could do about our wrapping the mortgages, the bank came up with this idea: If the real estate industry would let the bank handle the wrap-arounds, take charge, the only thing they wanted was to be allowed to raise the first mortgage by one percent. This only costs the seller one percent on his first mortgage (remember that he is making a profit on the first mortgage, in the above example, of six percent. He would only be getting five percent if the bank took over. We all loved that one. The bank would be in charge of all the paper-work, they would see to all the safeguards, etc. We were extremely happy with this new development. With the Magic Wrap the bank is the lender. The seller doesn't have to hold the mortgage and receives his cash up front, allowing him to pursue his dream. The buyer is able to purchase the house at below-market rates and will enjoy lower payments.

Low Interest Mortgage Discount way to buy a house. This one is for the seller, the owner of a first mortgage, who wants to buy a new home, but needs help in qualifying for the down payment on the new one. Although this one is "weak," I'm going to call it Number 44. If the seller has a low interest mortgage, say 10% or under, he may increase his equity position, perhaps enabling him to qualify for the down payment of that new house by asking for the discount upon closing out that low-rate loan. During high interest, stand-still-market interims, many banks sent out letters to their mortgagors (borrowers) that they would pay "X" amount of discount (as much as up to the neighborhood of 10 %!) to those owners who would pay off those old loans. My wife and I were paying a 7 ½% mortgage and got one of those letters from the bank. They would discount the mortgage if we would come in and pay them off. Are you kidding? We were struggling on the upkeep of four kids, three dogs (Surely, Goodness and Mercy), a cat and my mother-in-law, plus the mortgage! It never hurts to ask. People who do not ask for the discount close loans every day without receiving discounts. If it hasn't already been offered by the bank, it certainly won't be volunteered at the closing table. Ask for the discount. Always.

Number 45 is going to get the name State Housing Agency Loan. There are some forty states that have State Housing Authorities for purposes of assisting deserving people who qualify, in getting their first home. The buyer must be a first-time buyer, defined as one who has not had an ownership interest in a primary residence during the preceding three years. The property must be occupied as the buyer's primary residence. The purchase price of the property must be a price in excess of 90% of the median sales prices of homes in the area (there are different sales price limits for new and existing properties. In certain designated SMSA targeted areas, the first-time homebuyer restriction does not apply and the sales price may be as high as 110% of the median. All mortgages must be new and no refinancings are allowed. The loans are predominantly 30-year loans except for the possible inclusion of "buy-downs." Private Mortgage Insurance is required on "Conventional loans having a loan-to-value ratio greater than 80%, meaning 90's and 95's. Income limits vary from state SMSA to SMSA. These loans are not subsidies (handouts), but low-interest loans that must be paid back. Picture, if you will, a divorced parent, who is deserving, with kids, has a good job, is stable and who, with just a tiny push, can "get a leg up." That person can join the homeowners of America! To find out of your state has such an Authority, write to Council of State Housing Agencies, 1133 fifteenth St., N.W., Suite 514, Washington, D.C. 20005. They provide a directory. The several Authorities or Agencies get their authority from the respective state governments. Each agency has several boards who oversee, hinder, hamper, place obstacles, or facilitate them in their goal of making shelter obtainable. Federal legislation allows them to sell tax-free revenue bonds on the municipal bond market. A tax-free bond is one on which the owner (purchaser) of the bond) is exempt from paying taxes on the interest that the agency pays them. The bonds are low interest. So are the loans that the agency provides. Mortgage lenders apply and are approved to originate loans in the local markets. The funds are targeted to certain areas to insure uniform and equal distribution called SMSA (Standard Metropolitan Statistical Areas). Georgia, for example, has seven SMSA's, each containing from 2 to 15 counties. 60% of the USA population lives in a SMSA, the other 40%, outside. The state legislatures determine or earmark where the monies shall go. In Georgia GRFA (Georgia Residential Finance Authority) must earmark 40% of the monies to within SMSA, and 40% outside a SMSA. The remaining 20% is up to GRFA's discretion which is usually loaned out in a designated or targeted area which is generally economically poor or depressed within the SMSA. How boring and uninteresting!

Way Number 46, I call the "Funny" Way to Buy: most lending institutions, if not all of them, permit "co-borrowers" on loan applications for home purchases. In fact, federal regulations disallow certain types of discrimination. It is therefore possible for two "funny" persons to get together and share a house-purchase, both helping toward the overall qualifying. The reason I mention "funny" persons is that close-together-living circumstances demand a certain amount of compatibility in the sharing of a house. Notwithstanding, it is quite possible, and I have seen more than one family share a home that had two master bedrooms, one at each opposite end of the house. If harmony can be maintained long enough to realize enough equity buildup through payments and normal (or abnormal) appreciation, then they sell and split (no pun intended). Ideally, the equity shares would be enough for each to purchase his/her respective single residence. Compatibility is less important in the purchase of a duplex, triplex, etc., but there must be agreements as to <u>when</u> to sell and split and/or <u>how much</u> to split in order to avoid a stand-off or grudge-kill of a sale.

Way Number 47 is the Pledge Future Income Loan. There are many instances where a person (buyer) has an income stream that is a fixed amount, possible with built-in increases. For example, a net lease (a lease whereby the tenant pays an exact amount to the landlord, as well as pay all expenses, insurance, taxes, repairs), or payments from a pension fund, dividends from stock, such as preferred stocks, inheritance trust funds – any steady source of income which he may pledge it all or a portion over a specified time period as down payment. This enables you to buy <u>now,</u> getting in on lower prices, maybe even attractive interest rates. You close the transaction, receiving title to the property, move in and make regular payments. Your (purchaser's) bank deducts each month, a portion (draw) from your fixed income stream until your note for the down payment is satisfied. By pledging certain amounts, which the bank (third party) handles and disperses to the seller, he is sure of receiving his money on a regularly scheduled basis. Your house loan may be Conventional, FHA, VA or seller financed, whatever.

Another suggestion and an alternative to stable income stream: Suppose you (buyer) are assured of an inheritance that is forthcoming. Pledge it, or a part of it as down payment to acquire that house <u>now.</u>

Way Number 48, I will call Security Deposit Loan. There are many times that the bank would love to make a loan—the purchaser looks rather good, the house is good collateral, but for one reason or another, the loan falls into the category of maybe or probably not. Other customers have priority, quotas have been met, etc. The purchaser—borrower always takes it personal, whereas, in better times, he could have got the loan. In this case the seller offers to deposit, say, $10,000 as security (drawing interest, of course) until that amount of the loan is paid off. This is the same as insurance of the top portion of the loan (private mortgage insurance). Take this one step farther, or let's look at another set of circumstances: A purchaser can't afford, or doesn't want to pay more than 15% interest (suppose interest is at 17% or 18%). The seller doesn't need the cash equity of $50,000, so he leaves that amount that he realizes from the sale in his bank. That is called collateralizing (pledging as security) so that the bank will make the loan to the purchaser at the negotiated interest rate. The purchaser gets his 15% interest, the seller draws an attractive interest, the bank uses that sum and makes money on top of all this transaction and all's well that ends well.

Number 49 is Put Up The Car. Sometimes the purchaser almost qualifies for the loan, but, no loan! It could be that he tried to qualify for a high loan-to-value-ratio loan (95%) and used up all his cash. He has a good job, shows stability, his debt ratio is good—he's just short of savings. Put up the car as additional collateral. He may own stocks that could be offered as additional collateral. Not only is he proving worthy of the loan, but is enhancing the bank's position in the transaction. The more a person puts of himself into the transaction (cash down payment, security pledges), the less likely the bank will have to step in and take back the property. But, don't overdo it. If they only want the cat box, don't offer the cat too!

Number 50 is a little "lame," but it is, nonetheless, a way to buy a house. I call it Tap The Insurance. Most of us in these United States own insurance policies that have cash value. In fact, many of us are "insurance poor" (too much of a good thing). Hey, it's already your money! Why go out and borrow from someone else when you can borrow from yourself? Borrow against that insurance policy and become one of the Homeowners of America while you are still alive! Leave them a house (or two—three) when you "go!" There, you've got that down payment! Rush out and find the right buy.

Number 51 isn't that far-fetched either: Certificate of Deposit In Lieu Of Discount. We live in a very fast moving world where many jobs are subject to transfer out of town. Your employer needs for you to pack up and move to the "new" location pronto. They (your corporation) are usually willing, if not downright obligated, to pay the discount points on your new loan, among other things. Here is a way to save them thousands of dollars and get the same job done (get your loan through). Instead of paying the discount points (money down the drain), have them take out a large certificate of deposit (CD) at the bank where you are getting the financing. This way you are able to qualify more easily, the bank gets the use of the money, your company eventually gets all their money back—and then some.

Number 52 is also "lame," but a way to buy a house: Credit Union Loan. Large corporations usually have credit unions that make employee loans to purchase most anything, houses included. So, if you work at a place where there is a credit union, the interest rate to employees is usually much less than current market conditions, if not, at least it's available. Buy that home. They probably won't fire you either, at least not until you have paid them off (job security).

Number 53 is Seller Borrows Own Equity. This type of financing has been widely used and is quite well known by everyone in the housing industry—not that all the rest of these ways aren't either, -but for the uninformed, here goes: The seller wants to sell and has a buyer who hasn't yet established a rapport, or a line of credit due to being too young, fresh out of college—any number of things (short of cash). The seller goes to his bank and borrows enough to pay off the old loan and then some, or as much as he can get. Example in simple terms and numbers: The buyer has $20,000 cash. The sales price is $70,000, the first mortgage owed is $25,000, leaving an equity of $45,000. The seller goes out and borrows $50,000, making sure that this new loan is assumable (if not, remember the limited power of atty. that we talked about, etc.) From the $50,000 he takes $25,000 and pays off the first mortgage. This leaves him $25,000. The buyer has $20,000. This gives the seller all his equity of $45,000: Sales price $70,000, new first mortgage of $50,000, equity $20,000 that he has received from the purchaser. The purchaser begins payments on the $50,000 mortgage. If the purchaser doesn't have quite enough money to completely pay off the seller, as in the above example, then the seller takes back a small second mortgage.

It's time for a foreclosure update and a brief history class. Today, January, of 2009, there are 947 properties advertised to foreclose the second Tuesday of February on the Cobb County court house steps to the highest bidder! That's a record for all times. Gwinnett County, Georgia has more than 1150 this same month. Did you know that Abe Lincoln lost his home to foreclosure two times? That means he lost ingress and egress (exotic birds). His foreclosures weren't due to ARM's (Adjustable Rate Mortgages as most of ours are today. Though it is still available, even pushed by banks, and I will call Way number 54, stay away from the ARM. I hate it so much that I'm not even going to explain all the ins and outs to you. It is the bane of real estate. I'd rather write about the dangers of quicksand. Stay away from it! There are caps, both yearly and overall, but humans generally spend any extra money or "overages." The caps are based on agreed upon indexes such as Treasury securities, Treasury bills, etc. I call the ARM the GUM Mortgage (Goes Up Mortgage). I have never seen one go down! Once a person has adjusted to paying, say, $800.00 per month for his house payment, the rest of his salary he easily spends on other things (sometimes necessities). All of a sudden, one month, his house payment goes up by $400.00! That's hard to adjust to. Don't ever, ever, ever let a bank talk you into signing an ARM! Instead ask for a fixed rate mortgage, or some other instrument, anything but an ARM.

The History Class that I promised concerns Fannie Mae and some of the loans she will buy: AMI, ROM, VRM, RRM, ARM, GPM, GPAM, FLIP, FLEX, FPM, LPM, AND SAM loans. I plan to tell you about some of these individual loans (Ways) at the appropriate time later. Meet Fannie Mae (Federal National Mortgage Association). Fannie Mae was originally a government-owned entity. Under the 1968 housing Act, FNMA became a quasi-private corporation with the legal structure of a private corporate entity. It is a private shareholder-owned corporation and is the largest investor in our nation. It buys mortgage loans from local banks, savings and loan associations, mortgage corporations and other lenders. Did you also know that if you have your PMM (Purchase Money Mortgage—when the seller takes back a mortgage) originated on the proper paperwork, that FNMA will purchase your mortgage from you as well?

When she buys the mortgage from the lending institution, that lending institution then has the money to turn right around and lend out the money again (We aren't saving money fast enough for the banks to keep up with the lending demands). She is then a secondary mortgage market (not a 2nd mortgage market), although she will also purchase 2nd mortgages).

Once upon a time, FNMA decided that she wouldn't purchase fixed-rate mortgages unless the interest were high enough. She had been buying these fixed-rate mortgages with the market-interest climbing—she had been used to recouping all her money within about seven years. We real estate people and the public could not see letting the bank have back the low-interest mortgages (remember, under Carter, the interest went up to 21%!), so we would sell the house on a loan assumption with the seller's taking back a 2nd mortgage (PMM), or we would do a "Wrap-around" mortgage, over and over and again. FNMA required us to insert "Paragraph 17" into all loan papers or she wouldn't buy loans from Georgia. We capitulated immediately. Paragraph 17, was the due-on-sale clause. No more loan assumptions, so they thought. Remember, Fans, the Limited Power Of Attorney? Anyway, the paragraph 17 was supposed to prohibit conveying any interest in the property without written permission from the lender. That includes renting the property. It also means that you may not remodel without their approval. That makes sense, though. You might destroy the collateral for the loan. Imagine when Martha tells Ralph "Hun, lets tear out these three walls and make one great big master bedroom. We can then run naked and throw ice water." Ralph likes the idea and they tear out three walls, making theirs a one-bedroom, two-bath house that is obsolete in the market. They also probably tore out a load bearing wall at the same time. The collateral has been destroyed as far as the bank is concerned. Anyway, with that paragraph inserted in all of Georgia's loan papers, FNMA then became happy again and began making profits. I won't go into the tribulations of FNMA during 2008—you already know that sad story, banks were ordered to extend credit to people undeserving of such and those same people lost their houses, ARM's, deflation, etc. I do take exception with most of one of those reasons, specifically the undeserving loans. I teach (taught) real estate classes. I taught students (real estate agents) how to qualify their people for loans. I am not personally aware of any person (buyer) nor agent in my realm of real estate, who participated in the above. My people earn their commissions ethically and legally, the way they were taught. Apparently, FNMA and Freddie Mac, deserved their woes due to all that disgusting behavior. Enough said on the subject!

Way Number 55: The Roll - Over Mortgage (ROM) provided for the renegotiation of the interest rate at regular intervals of 3-7 years. Interest rates were adjusted within limits based on a predetermined index. The maximum up or down was 5% over the life of the mortgage.

Way Number 56 is The Variable Rate Mortgage (VRM) was the first residential mortgage that offered an interest rate that could be adjusted up or down. It was meant to reflect the cost of funds and that was calculated from a national index of costs for the savings and loan associations. The rate could go up at the lender's discretion while downward adjustments were mandatory. Interest could be adjusted once a year but the maximum was one half percent. There was a ceiling on increases over the life of the loan of 2 ½ % upward. The interest was usually lower than that charged for a fixed-rate loan. There were many disadvantages to the Savings and Loan associations, such as having to disclose "worst case" scenarios (tell how high your payments would be if worse came to worse). While similar to the above ROM, the interval between adjustments were shorter in the VRM.

Way Number 57 is The Renegotiable Rate Mortgage (RRM) were loans made for a term of either three, four or five years, but amortized over 30 years. Federal banks had to renew the loan at the end of the term. State chartered S&Ls, commercial banks and other lenders did not have to. At the end of every period, one renegotiated the interest rate with the lender, up or down. The amount and interval was pre-determined by the lender. If you chose not to renegotiate the loan at the new terms, you must then and there, pay them off. The loan might have a seven-year call—they wanted all their money back in seven years. The RRMs were very popular with customers because of the relatively low interest rates. Also the interest couldn't increase more than ½ % per year. There was a 5% upward adjustment limit over the life of the mortgage. The adjustments occurred less frequently on the RRMs but if the rate was adjusted to the full 5% limit, the payments could increase by 50%. S&Ls liked this one. They didn't have to disclose the "worst case" scenario. The Federal Home Loan Bank Board now prohibits the S&Ls from making RRMs because they lose money on them. Private investors may still make them. Lines do not form though.

Way Number 58 is The FLEX—flexible payment mortgage/Variable Rate Mortgages allow the bank to adjust the length of the payment period, change the rate, based on an index, etc. Here a person is qualified to purchase based on expected future income stream. Not bad for some people, secure in their jobs. Enough said about all of these.

Way Number 59 is The GPM (Graduated Payment Mortgage) is nothing more than one of the five FHA-245 series. Low payments in the early years with the unpaid amounts added to the loan—negative amortization—only recommended in times of good/large inflation. I used to sell $60,000 houses to people who could only afford payments on a $40,000 home. It is called negative amortization—the FHA-245 program. It still exists and is a viable way to own a house. Not recommended unless there is healthy inflation. As you make payments in the early years that are lower than they should be, the unpaid overage is simply added to the loan. It is like a snowball, always growing as it rolls. If there is enough inflation (increase in home values), after a time, the inflation has outrun the snowball, creating equity. This was a fantastic program at one time. You bought for $60,000. At the end of five years, say, the house is worth $75,000. The loan, which has been increasing, is now up to $65,000. You have $10,000 because of inflation. In the first two years, (the once-upon-a-time basis for the 245 Program) the buyer has received raises in his job, enabling him to make the regular "$60,000" payments that he couldn't pay earlier.

Way number 60, is called Level Payment Plan. It is also an ARM!!!! Here both features of fixed-rate and flexible mortgages are combined. You get the security of constant monthly payments and the lender can adjust the interest rate a couple times each year. The payments remain the same. When the rates rise, a greater portion goes to interest. When the rates drop, the principal is paid off quicker. There was one catch. These loans allowed for resetting the payment amount every three to five years. This would assure that it was high enough to amortize the loan. Here, the uneducated sign up for a mortgage that has a level payment. Young buyers seem to like that. It is a negative amortization plan where the mortgage keeps growing. However, if there is no corresponding faster-growing inflation, the snowball loan gets bigger than the value and then, if the homeowner wanted to sell, he's have to borrow money above the price of his home to be able to pay off the mortgage. The lender doesn't have to explain the negative on this one. Avoid this one. Please, always ask for a FIXED RATE MORTGAGE. Thank you! If you are now in one of these ARMs, convert to a fixed rate ASAP. Have you ever heard of Foreclosure Ville? Remember what happened to Abe Lincoln? Ingress and Egress?

Let me finish with Fannie Mae's ways that she would buy mortgages from banks. She had eight ARMs that she would purchase: Way Number 61 is Plan One. The index as a 6-month Treasury Bill. The adjustment period was six months. There was no Interest Rate Cap. Principal and Interest payments had a cap of 7 ½%. At five-year intervals the payments were reset without regard to the 7.5% cap.

Way Number 62 is Plan Two. The index was a six month Treasury Bill, adjusted every three years, no interest rate cap, etc. Payment remained constant for three years, based on the interest rate the lender projected the interest to be over that period. If the payments were insufficient, the overage was added to the loan—negative amortization, of course.

Way Number 63 is Plan Three. The index was one year Treasury securities, one year adjustment period at the borrower's option, with any additional increase added to the loan principal up to 125%! of the original loan amount. Every five years the payments were reset without regard to the 7.5% cap to fully amortize the remaining balance.

Way Number 64 is Plan Four. The index was the 3-year Treasury Securities, adjusted every 2 ½ years, no interest cap, the principle and interest payment cap was 18 ¾ % (7.5 each year times 2 ½ years) each adjustment period, with negative amortization up to 125% of original loan. Every five years the payments were reset without regard to the 18 ¾ % cap to fully amortize the balance.

Tired already? I am too. I'll just mention the remaining four plans: Way Number 65 is Plan Five—index 3-year Treasury Securities, 2 ½ year period. Way Number 66 is Plan Six—5-year index. Way Number 67 is Plan Seven. The index– Federal Home Loan Bank "Board Series for Loans Recently Closed Homes, one year adjustment. And finally, Way Number 68 is Plan Eight—Index- Federal Home Loan Bank Board Series for Loans Recently Closed on Existing Homes, one-year adjustment with a Rate Cap of 2% up or down each adjustment period. If the index had increased or decreased by more than 2%, the additional increase or decrease might be carried over to subsequent adjustment periods unless there had been an offsetting move in the index.

Way Number 69 is The Graduated Payment Adjustable Mortgage (GPAM). It is available only in some state-chartered banks in California, but need to be mentioned here to be complete in my reporting. Instead of negative amortization, a savings account is set up by you, your relatives, your employer, or the preacher. Monthly draws from this account subsidize the monthly payments. The account is usually depleted between 2 – 5 years. The size of the account depends on the draws needed to subsidize the monthly payments.

Way Number 70 is The Flexible Loan Insurance Program (FLIP). It is set up so that a portion of the down payment goes to reduce payments in the early years of the loan. There is no negative amortization. Again, a savings account is set up by you, a relative or employer. Monthly draws from the account subsidize the monthly payments. The FLIP is still possible, to my knowledge.

Way Number 71 is the Flexible Payment Mortgage (FPM). You pay interest-only on the loan the first five years of the loan. The loan is then amortized on a regular basis for a maximum of 35 years. Some people combine this mortgage with the buy-down, already mentioned. This mortgage is good for some people, of course, depending on their circumstances.

Way Number 72 is the Urban Rehabilitation Program. Most metropolitan areas, at one time or another, offer houses for $1.00 each. It is done by drawing usually, but in some cases by bid. The purchaser must be willing to live in the house and show that he possesses adequate funds to improve, refurbish, or downright make livable the $1.00 house. This program has turned many declining areas of cities into nice neighborhoods. The municipality sometimes offers the buyers low-interest loans for rehabilitation. I would suggest that you check with your local administration to see if such a plan is available.

Way Number 73 is Cut Gems and Diamonds sale. I had only one occasion to participate in one of these. One should know what one is doing, especially the seller, if one participates in this sort of arrangement. The purchaser wishes to pay for the property in a lump sum of cut gems/and or diamonds. I watched as one of my sellers held in her hands $10,000 worth of diamonds as the down payment. They surely glittered! That particular sale finally fell through because the purchaser on a "lease/purchase could not or did not come up with the final amount. There is a big caveat. The value of the diamonds is, in my humble opinion, questionable. This group that I came upon, I shall call them some sort of Mafia. They would always check the phone to see if it were bugged. They kept asking me about our phone lines. But, they had the diamonds! They also had the diamond appraisers! It seemed that they owned or controlled both. I was told that diamonds appraised at $10,000 would only bring about one third of that price on the market. Hey, what good is an appraisal? At any rate, they said that they would "squash" the value, meaning that they would give three times the appraised value of the diamonds, in diamonds, of course. Also, they seem to own the diamond minds. My seller was told all this. She still wanted those diamonds! My broker, at that time, wouldn't allow me to collect the commission in diamonds. Shoot! I wanted them too! The seller would have to pay the commission in cash. However, in a lease/purchase we real estate people only get paid at closing, and that never happened—I got a lot of experience and the seller kept the beautiful diamonds—down payment. It is, however, a Way to purchase property. The conversion of gems and stock into dollars can be difficult as well as costly unless a person has expertise. The many sales daily across the country involving gems requires sophisticated participants—persons <u>not</u> living from hand to mouth (no cash flow)—persons not expecting to convert the gems into immediate cash. Just the mention of this kind of sale—diamonds, emeralds rubies, sapphires, etc, sends me into regal thoughts of kings, sultans, power-people—got rocks! Pun intended.

Though there are many programs, and I have given you a few, I am going to assign Programs, way Number 74. I personally don't approve of government programs as they usually cost tax-payers money. However, some don't. For example, the Kiddie Condo Loan is a program in that the down payment is only 3%, where usually, the down payment for FHA fits into one of two categories: those houses $50,000 and below to those more than $50,000. So long as the buyer can qualify for and repay the loan, I have no qualms about a Program. Fannie Mae had 8 ARM plans, not including the 5 FHA plans. I omitted some of them from my notes. What you must do to find out about what plans are available is to ask any loan officer from your bank or mortgage company.

If there should be a new program for left-handed lesbians, then I want to know about it. Did you know that you can always tell a left-handed person? You can't tell them much.

Way number 75 is Trading Stocks for real estate. I am not talking about the cattle kind of stock, although that might work too. It takes a willing buyer and a willing seller in all transactions. The conversion of gens and stock into dollars can be difficult as well as costly unless a person has expertise. If you can trade stock for more than you paid for it, you made a profit. If you trade at par, what you paid for it, you didn't gain—on your stock. If you have to trade below what you paid for the stock, then you traded at a loss. But, what you gained in the trade, be you the seller or the buyer, is the end result. Each thinks he gained and he is probably right.

Way Number 76 is the Reverse Annuity Mortgage (RAM)/ Private Insurance Annuity. There are so many different kinds, variations and forms that books have been written on the subject. I shall give you some basics as to how I perceive their role in the real estate industry. An annuity is an investment that yields fixed payments, especially yearly payments (annual annuity), but may also be received monthly. Payments are determined by reference to complicated, standard annuity tables. An annuity that involves transferring property to a member of the family, when structured by a qualified person, can produce savings in taxes (gift taxes, income tax, estate tax). This mortgage is popularly known as simply the Reverse Mortgage. This mortgage allows homeowners, the elderly, to receive monthly payments on the equity that they have in their home. The loan is paid back on a specified date or upon the sale of the property or the death of the borrower. A reverse mortgage is a great way for the elderly to down-purchase—buy a smaller home, cheaper home, move to Florida! A lot of thought needs to go into this one by consulting specialists, so that the borrower is protected.

Way Number 77 is the Absolute Auction. In an "absolute" auction, the highest bidder, no matter how small, gets the property at that bid. The highest bid could be $1,000 on a home worth $150,000! Remember, the highest bidder gets the property. At all auctions they want 10% down—that day and you usually are given twenty-four hours to pay the balance. All auctioneers have their different rules. I found out that Auctioneers don't co-op their sales. I wanted to share in the 10% commission on a house that my wife and I bought. No way, José. You should check with local auctioneers and the newspapers as to when and where these auctions take place. Even if the auction is not "absolute," bargains are to be had at almost every one of them.

Way Number 78 is the Advance Payments Deposit. Not everyone in the world, who is trying to get a house, is flat broke. Some people don't have to worry about a source of funds—let's say they have a nest egg. But, neither do you want something or someone messing around with your eggs! You may have a savings and still the bank won't make the loan. In that case, offer to make all the first year's payments with a lump sum deposit. The bank gets to use the money and you don't lose your interest. You get the loan, the house, and the interest of that nest egg. Don't be chintzy with the money! You have to pay it anyway! It hurts the puppy more to bob his tail an inch at a time than to get it all over at once. And in this case you benefit all around.

Way Number 79 is the Equity Advance. There actually are real estate companies that will advance to you certain percentages of the equity (up to 80%) in order for you to purchase (loan assumption) a home. You give them a note with interest. If they can afford it, if you are a good risk, the house a good investment (always), it is a way to keep the market on the move. It doesn't hurt to ask! When you ask, should the agent throw his/her hands over his/her mouth and rush out of the room—he/she had to find a private place to laugh—that particular real estate company doesn't offer that particular program!

Way Number 80 involves the real estate company as in the above plan. This Way is the Guaranteed Sales Plan. The real estate company lists your house (you understand what "lists" means, don't you? When you list a house, you make it lean like the Tower of Pisa!), and you enter into a contract to purchase a house (generally new home) from them. They promise that if your present house hasn't sold by the time you are to close on the new one, they will purchase your old home from you. Builders like this one because they are moving inventory. The real estate company benefits by pleasing the builder and collects commissions on two transactions. Let it be known that the real estate company doesn't want your house. They have to turn around and sell it to recoup their money. Selling the house is expensive. The costs: 7% real estate commission, 3% holding time (house payments), 3% repairs (perchance), 3.3% closing costs (it is always easier to sell a house by offering to pay these costs), 2 ½% PMI (it is always easier to offer to pay this cost), there might be discount points to pay —we are already up to around 20% costs! The State of Georgia passed a law that, in the case of a guaranteed sale plan, the real estate company must, at the time of listing the house, present to the homeowner the actual sales contract on the present home. It was a disclosure law. If a homeowner listed his house for $100,000, thinking that the company was going to pay him that amount so that he could purchase the new one, what a surprise then the company offered him 21% ($79,000) less for the purchase price of his old house. Remember, he is already under contract to purchase a new one! The new Georgia law keeps everyone above board. It would have cost the homeowner the same 21% if he sold it himself in the same ideal conditions.

In Way Number 31, I mentioned the Straight Note or Interest Only Loan way to purchase a house. I would be remiss if I didn't tell you about Way Number 81, the Balloon Note. It is so much like the above mentioned Ways. The purchaser plans to live in the new home a relatively short time. The differences in this loan and the RRM, is that in the RRM the interest is renegotiated. The Balloon Note is paid off when the note becomes due. Also different from Way Number 24 Single Payment Note where you pay no interest nor principal until the note is due. In a Balloon Note, and they are quite common, one pays regular monthly payments that have been amortized as though it were a thirty-year loan, you are paying principal and interest. When the note becomes due, you pay off the whole thing. Again, insist on a Prepayment Privilege/Or More clause. Back in the 1920s and early 1930s the Balloon and the Straight note were the most common, if not, the only mortgages available. The Great Depression came along and this mortgage became known as the Lose-Everything-You-Own or the Blow-Your-Head-Off mortgage. When that big last payment came along and people couldn't pay, they did indeed lose everything. It was not so much that banks wouldn't renegotiate the loan, they weren't allowed to. This caused a flood of foreclosures and is one of the primary reasons for the birth of FHA.

Way Number 82 is the Blanket Mortgage. A blanket mortgage is one that is secured by more than one piece of property. If you buy a house and the adjacent lot, a blanket mortgage would include both pieces of property. But, you can buy property using a blanket mortgage to help acquire it. Simply, if you already own another piece of property and if the equity in the extra property is high enough, both may be enough to stand as security for the new property. The bank will place one mortgage collateralized (secured) by both properties. You normally would seek to have a "release clause" so that when you have paid, say, up to 110% of the value of the second property, the bank will release it from being held as security. You wouldn't want some unseen catastrophe to cause you to lose both in a foreclosure. When a builder purchases acreage, he usually obtains a blanket mortgage with a release clause. The bank holds title to all the lots under the mortgage. With a release clause, the builder may develop individual lots, have them releases to him so that he can give clear title to his buyers.

Way Number 83 is a Package Mortgage. Mobile homes/Trailers are usually purchased with a package mortgage. Oh, you don't like the term "Trailer?" OK, some people call them "Manufactured Housing." If it has feathers, waddles, and quacks, it is probably a Duck! The Manufactured housing came in on a "trailer." Remove the wheels, even though they are wire wheels, it is still a trailer. Back to the Package Mortgage, it simply means that not only real estate is covered in the mortgage, but also personalty—the washer, dryer, refrigerator, stove and perchance the furniture—all financed along with the realty. It doesn't necessarily have to be a "manufactured housing." Banks have found that purchasers can more easily afford the payments in a package which includes almost everything—(budget mortgage) includes taxes, insurance, etc.—than having to exhaust his/her resources by paying cash for these items, or financing them at add-on rates. In a package mortgage you only pay interest on the loan balance, not on the original debt as is usual in a consumer installment loan. Your payments will include principal and interest and prorate payments for the appliances. In the long run, the refrigerator will cost two times as much as a cash sale would, but, it is easier to pay smaller payments for a longer period of time and not have the added risk of losing everything you own by getting up-to-your-eyeballs in debt to pay for the refrigerator separately.

Way Number 84 is the FLEXIBLE FIXED RATE MORTGAGE. This mortgage offers/offered the borrower the security of a fixed rate, yet it gave the lender a rate of return that could rise as the costs of funds rose. It was a variable rate insurance program. The buyer got a mortgage at current rates, say, 15%. If the rate dropped below that percentage, the lender enjoyed his bonus return. If the rate went up beyond the 15%, the insurance reimbursed the bank for the difference in return between the loan made at the original fixed rate and the one made at current market rate, or a maximum rate prescribed by the insurance program, whichever was the lowest. One half percent per year over the life of the loan was added to the original rate excluding year one. A fifteen percent mortgage would be fully covered from loss for ten years even if the mortgage rate rose to 19 ½%. The one-time premium was tied to the selling price of the home whose mortgage was insured with ranges from 1 ½% to 9% of the selling price. Thirty states' insurance commissions approved this program and it was filed in all 50 states. How boring, right?

Way Number 85 is an excellent way to become a homeowner. It is probably a Cheetah for some folks. It is to Move A House To Your Lot. You need to buy a vacant lot—cheaper than buying a house! Many folks will give you the house if you will move it. Municipalities will give it to you if they are undergoing Urban Renewal. They and private parties either need to demolish it, burn it, or move it. Of course there is some expense to moving a house, but there are companies that specialize in just that. All you need do is get the permits to hook up the utilities, etc., do some minor adjusting and you have your starter home—maybe even your dream house. It certainly beats paying rent to someone else. Keep making to yourself those equivalent tent payments into your savings account to save up to buy your real dream house.

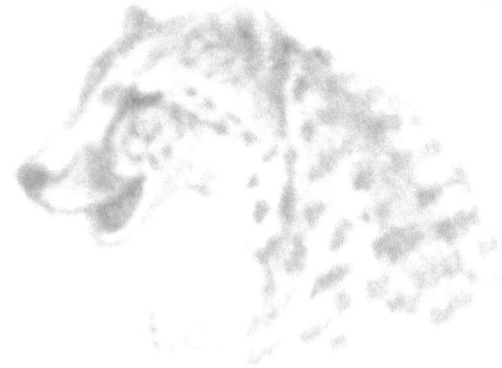

Way Number 86—The Adobe. When I was around ten years old, we went to visit an aunt in Buena Vista, New Mexico. While out there, I watched some neighbors build an adobe house. They (the workers were all Mexican) made bricks by mixing mud and straw. The "hole" later would be the cellar. They made a form that would hold around six bricks. They would pour the mix into the form and then shake it out to dry in the sun. Then they filled it up again. What an idea! I always wanted to build one, but my house is too nice to start all over again. There are plenty of illegal aliens running around with this knowledge. They don't even have to be illegal. Go for it! For some of you, starting out, that one is a Cheetah!

Way Number 87 is the FHA 234 Plan. The word Condominium is a French word meaning "You paid too much for it." All FHA condominiums for this program must be approved by FHA. This Plan 234 is for brand new condos: they are either being built or being converted over, such as an apartment, etc.

Way Number 88 is almost a waste of a Way Number, but since it exists and is legit, I offer it. It is the Existing Condo. To purchase it you simply ask for the FHA 203b Plan. This plan is the most popular one. It is a "Program" different from the standard FHA Ways I already told you about. This one has a down payment of only about 1.25%

Way Number 89 is the FHA/VA Combo Plan. This plan came into being for veterans who had already used-up their entitlement so that they could still benefit from being a veteran. A word here about used up entitlement. In the past, the entitlement, as I have already told you, was increased by congress from time to time. When It was $30,000, that meant that a veteran could buy a house costing four times that--$120,000. Back then VA loans were assumable (We have met the Cheetah that _all_ loans are now assumable, remember?—Limited power of atty.). Suppose a veteran had sold his home on a loan assumption. He lost some of his entitlement on this formula: Sixty percent times the original sales price equals the amount of entitlement he has used up. That formula still applies today. So, if he had paid $30,000 for his house, he had used up $18,000 of entitlement, leaving him $12,000 of entitlement—times four—he could purchase a house valuing, unless he paid the overage, $48,000. Not many houses selling at that price except maybe in Mexico. Again, once the veteran's previous loan is repaid, his lost entitlement is restored automatically. Well, back to the Combo FHA/VA plan: Take the sales price, times 5% and subtract $1,200. This becomes the veteran's down payment. You see, this is $700 cheaper than the regular FHA financing and $1,200 cheaper than going Conventional 95%. Go, Veterans!

Way Number 90 is the Tax FIFA Purchase. I personally think that this is a sleazy way to buy a house, so I call it the Sleazebag way. There are "people" at the court house at this very moment and on a daily basis, looking up delinquent real estate taxes. If someone is delinquent in paying his taxes (Democrat Cabinet Nominees) on his real estate, one can go and pay (buy) the tax FIFA and foreclose on it at the required (in your state) period. That person usually had one year (equitable time of redemption) to pay up plus penalties, etc., and reclaim his property.

Some folks think that one can just pay up at any time and reclaim the property—not! The one losing the property through foreclosure has the same right to go to the foreclosure sale and bid on it for cash just like everybody else! The only redemption period that exists, to my knowledge, is a Tax Sale (foreclosure). These people generally have one year to reclaim. Also, if a person signs a contract to purchase real property, he can't die out of the contract, can't go berserk out of it, if it burns down before closing, it floats off down the creek, he has still bought a vacant lot! (Should have insured it. In fact, it is recommended that as soon as you sign a real estate purchase contract, that you insure the property. You have equitable title, insurable. Remember, there's no cold foot law for real estate purchases). That also goes for the seller. It is sold! There is no 72-hour Cold Foot Law for real estate. The Cold Foot Law allows a person 72 hours to back out of any contract that would place a lien on your property—72 hours. Because of the Time Share industry—who use pressure tactics, Georgia's legislature passed a law allowing a person seven days to back out of any Condominium type sale, including condominiums, town houses, time share—seven days after all paperwork, which means closing. The state of Florida (lots of time share down there) allows ten days to back out of a Condo-type sale.

Way Number 91 is to simply Outbid At Foreclosure. Every county has a local paper for advertizing legal ads wherein they advertize all the legal notices such as foreclosures. They (in Georgia) must advertize for four consecutive weeks and then on the following week, at the courthouse, at public outcry, they sell to the highest bidder. If the lender is advertizing the property's delinquency of $32,000, and if there are no other higher bidders, the lender takes title to the property at that time. You come to the sale and offer $32,001, the property is yours. Again, the loser—(losee?) has the same right to buy his property back at that sale. In Georgia they advertize four times per month (Fridays papers) and the first Tuesday of the next month have the foreclosure up at the court house steps.

Way Number 92 is the Weekly and the Bi-Weekly Mortgage. A Cheetah here? Canada began this program years ago and it spread to the USA and caught on. Instead of making 12 monthly payments, you make 24 bi-weekly or 48 weekly payments. Each payment contains a little more principal and therefore shortens the 30-year mortgage term to around 18 to 21 years, drastically reducing the interest costs. Here in the USA,

some banks, on the bi-monthly mortgage, if the borrower missed two payments, then the entire mortgage would revert to the standard 30-year—twelve monthly payments—a regular level-payment annuity plan. The advantages to the borrower: a quicker build-up of equity, interest savings in the long run, the house is paid-for sooner, easier to budget (especially for someone on a weekly salary—easier than one big monthly payment). One easy way to set this up is for the bank to pay the mortgage from a weekly draw. Drawbacks: there is increased paperwork for the bank, although now that everything is computerized, that isn't such a drawback as it used to be.

Cheetah time again, Buckaroos! Way Number 93, using Government Bonds to purchase real estate. I got this idea from an article by Wayne Schultz and Arthur Carmano, circa 1986. Aren't you glad I kept notes? I am, hence this book! You buy bonds at a discount, say, you pay 75 cents on the dollar. Buy a government bond to mature in ten years. The bond pays interest on the face amount, not on what you paid for it. The seller wants $100,000 sales price. He will take back a PMM (purchase money mortgage) for, say, $25,000—ten year pay off, leaving you, the purchaser, to get a loan of $75,000 which the property will stand for. You give the seller the $25,000 cash from the proceeds of the loan, leaving you with $50,000 cash with which to buy the bond, say, $75,000 (all this fluctuates with the bond market, interest rates, etc.). You will pay the seller twenty payments of $2,625—or $52,500 over the ten-year period. The rent from the property pays the bank loan off. The interest from the bond pays the seller (20 payments). The seller is getting $52,500, $25,000—($77,500), leaving $22,500, which he will get as a lump sum in ten years. You buy the bond at closing, giving a receipt to the seller's lawyer. You can guarantee the seller's money because it is backed by a government bond that the seller's lawyer holds, but the bond pays you. The bond matures and the government sends you a check for $75,000. You pay the seller his $22,500, leaving you $52,500 cash tax-free. Interest on government bonds is not taxable. You have the house plus $52,500. The lien is on the bond, not the house, which the seller's lawyer holds. How slick can you get? Slick--not slickee. Slick is good. Slickee should go to jail. You will need a real estate accountant on this one.

I mentioned to you Slickee. I always told my classes that there were three kinds of real estate agents: Ding-a-ling, who never gets referrals, Slickee, who needs to be in jail, and we are catching him on a regular basis, and then there is the Pro. I teach the Pro. You are very fortunate when you get one of my agents/students! You are in good hands. That's why this book is dedicated to them and their success. You'll always find them over in the left lane!

Way Number 94 Annuities (Life Insurance). Many of you have a life insurance annuity—you paid a lump sum for an insurance policy that pays you an annual annuity for life. You are guaranteed this income for life. Males and females receive different amounts and percentages, but there are tables available that spell this out. Your annuity may be enough to make the house payments. Of course, those involved already know this, but, there could be a Cheetah in here for some of you who forgot. Watch as someone of you goes out and buys a house today using an annuity.

Way Number 95 is the Builder SAM (shared appreciation mortgage). No, his name isn't Sam. Sometimes, though, there comes that time when it is hard for the builder (Sammy) to move the inventory. Approach him with the idea of reducing the sales price—enabling you to be able to finance. Agree that he can recoup his (reduction) in the future, and at an agreed upon date. He wasn't foreclosed on (commercial loans—builder loans have very high interest rates, short terms. I don't know how builders get any sleep with that interest time-clock ticking off the dollars. He was hereby able to pay off the construction loan and be able to get another one. His profit will come later.

Way Number 96 is the RPM (Rapid Payoff Mortgage). This mortgage is good for the buyer who has come into some money, maybe from the resale of his previous home. This is similar to the Straight Note, but can be from five to fifteen years duration and is one that FNMA will buy. So often today, banks are offering buyer the 15-year mortgage—exactly one half the term of the regular 30-year mortgages. On a personal note, when I found out what my monthly payments would be for thirty years—and it was the absolute limit we could afford, if someone had dared offer me a fifteen year mortgage, I would have hit him in the mouth!, thinking, of course that the payments would double. In reality, the "extra" above a thirty-year loan is negligible, and the interest is lower, substantially lower. Worth looking into!

Way Number 97 FNMA Refinancing Plan. FNMA will refinance a loan if they already own that loan in their inventory up to 95% if you live in the house. They will only go 80% if you are an investor. You may use the proceeds for anything you wish—a new/different home.

Way Number 98 is another Cheetah! Duplex, Triplex, or Four Unit. If you plan to live there-in, renting out the other apartments, thereby paying the mortgage you will have caught the Cheetah by the tail! Zoning in many subdivisions only allow single family housing. In other words—no duplexes allowed. You may live in such a subdivision. How many Mexicans can you get into three bedrooms? Oops, excuse me! There is a way to get around the No-Duplex zoning. I'm not trying to get you into trouble, but sometimes there are situations when a person needs to do certain things in a different manner: Here's how a neighbor of mine seems to have got around the zoning, legally!! He refinished his basement into an apartment, moved into it and rented out the upstairs. Looks to me like a duplex, right? Not! Well, some folks (not I—I just sat back and enjoyed the show) got upset and called Code Enforcement to do something. Code Enforcement drove by and seeing no improvements, they left. Pressure brought them back out and they were compelled to go inside the home. There was a stairwell from the basement to the upper floor with padlocks on both sides of the door. Code Enforcement proclaimed that since there was an openable door, that there was "free access," therefore it was not a duplex. In a duplex there can be no free access. Had the owner closed off and sealed that door, perchance using sheetrock, etc, it would have been converted into a duplex. The zoning "Single Family" applies to <u>construction</u> and <u>not</u> how many families are allowed to occupy. That house is still going strong in our neighborhood. If your builder wants to build a mother-in-law suite, all he has to do is provide access—despite how many padlocks you can nail up. Oh, you don't know what a mother-in-law suite is? Well, you simply lower the ceiling in the crawl-space, using the finest asbestos available, and move her in……..

Way Number 99 is the Graduated Equity Mortgage or GEM. This is a mortgage that is amortized over thirty years but the payments increase each year based on the inflation rate. FNMA will purchase about six different plans with different interest rates and payoff dates. The increased payments (the overage) goes to pay down the principal, making that 30-year loan paid off in around twelve to fourteen years. There is a large savings in interest over the life of the loan. The buyer agrees to at least five years of increased (inflation-based) payments. This equity build-up, of course, makes it easier to buy the next house upon resale, or refinance.

Way Number 100 is the Zero Interest Financing. A builder needs to sell inventory. The buyer will need to pay at least thirty percent down payment. The balance of seventy percent will be equally divided into five-year payments (12 per year) at no interest—all principal. The payments are not too much more than the regular thirty-year amortized loan payments, and the house is paid off in five years, saving a couple hundred thousand dollars in interest—If you borrow $100,000, thirty years, you are going to eventually pay them $300,000 over the life of the loan. To make the builder's return on his investment palatable, increase the price of the house slightly—not too much out of line. You get the house with around the same payment, paid off in five years, the builder unloaded inventory, etc., enough said!

Way Number 101, and, for this book, the final Way, is to offer something that the Seller wants or needs. I have already mentioned boats and things in other Ways, but this method is suddenly growing across the nation. First, I will say that sellers got this ball rolling because it is presently, at the first of 2009, a buyers' market. That means that a buyer will have up to 20 houses to choose from. Sellers, recently, have been offering to pay the buyers' credit card debt to entice them to purchase their home. They even offer new cars! Well, all of this can work both ways, and since this book is how to buy a house, let's suggest a few things for the buyer to offer the seller to entice him to sell to them at a negotiated price. First, there should be a seller's market—a scarcity of houses to choose from—maybe not, you slick-tongue devil. Anyway, the market is ever-changing from sellers market to buyers' market. I remember when in California, people were selected by lottery to be able to bid on a house. Great for sellers.

For the buyer to entice the seller, perchance a new car. Maybe you have an extra one. Owning a home beats paying rent! Things you may offer, and you need to use your imagination, include Time Share, free trips, boat, car, credit card payoff, sky miles—for sellers—furniture. Folks, that is happening all over the country, especially today, since we are experiencing a buyer's market.

I have given you 101 ways—ideas to get a house. Don't go worrying to much and exacerbate the problem. Exacerbation happens to be legal in Georgia. Simply take one step at a time, get help, use the available professionals and you will be successful.

The following is not a Way, but I would be remiss if I didn't mention another mode of living. Before Columbus discovered America, the Indians lived in hogans, caves and Tipis (That's the correct spelling.). A book by Laubin and Laubin tells how to construct a tipi. My wife and I did so, so that I could go deer-hunting in it. We made a faithful reproduction of the Sioux tipi with one Cheyenne modification.... She wouldn't chew the buffalo hides, so we used Dacron for the shell. It is (inside) eighteen feet by twenty. Sleeps nine. It is cool in the summer and warm in the winter. Every summer, we would pack up the station wagon, tipi on top, all the animals, and head to St. Joseph Park at Port St. Joe, Florida for an affordable vacation. Our kids thought it was the most natural thing, camping for a week or two in the tipi. The smoke curls straight up and out the smoke-flaps hole. When it rains you simply close the smoke flaps. There's no running water—you have to run get it. Do you think I am suggesting that you live in a tipi while building a house? Naaaw. We take our tipi to "Indian powwows," scheduled often and we usually win the tipi competition, probably because we were faithful in our reproduction of the Indian tipi. Had an Indian, bless his heart, tell us that he hated Columbus. Yeah, he hated him for discovering America. Same Indian was extremely proud of his horse, saying "An Indian is nothing without his horse!" Hey, Tonto, guess who brought over the horses? Columbus brought them. We have in museums, pictures depicting the American Indian before Columbus (BC). The paintings invariably show the Indian lazing around with his horses....Not.

Closing costs, in closing…pun intended. Closing costs can be large or small, depending on the kind of sale. If the sale involves a loan from a lending institution, the costs are great. If you assume or get seller financing, or pay cash, the costs are minimal. I once asked a closing lawyer why they charge more to close on a large loan than on a small one. He responded."James, why do you get paid more on a large house than on a small one?" I learned to shut up. I think it was the same lawyer to whom I told a little, bitty, minor, lawyer joke. He responded: "James, do you know how to tell if a real estate agent is lying?…His mouth is open!" Not funny! Many of us think that Lawyer jokes are funny. Lawyers don't think so. They think that they are true! I happen to collect lawyer jokes..They no longer use rats for experiments in labs. They use lawyers…There's so many of them…You don't get attached to them…There are just some things a rat won't do. Being from Alabama, I don't think Alabama jokes are funny…A tornado hit the capitol of Alabama knocking it two feet off its wheels…and at the same time made $8,000,000 worth of improvements…An Alabamian invented the tooth brush. Had anyone else invented it, it would have been called the Teeth Brush…unfunny!

Closing attorneys are the real estate industry's best friends. You find yourself a good lawyer…Oops, oxymoron, efficient lawyer and you will be blessed. If the sale involves a cash sale, loan assumption, seller financing, the closing costs should be under or around $500. Here you are paying for a limited title search, always get title insurance, and then just the paperwork. If the sale included a PMM (seller takes back a second/purchase money mortgage), then there will be a charge for intangible taxes. There will be the charge for the hazard insurance policy and your share of taxes. In an institutional, new loan closing, the cost, in addition to the above, include percentages of the loan—lawyer fee, origination fee (bank charge), if the loan is greater than 80%, PMI, and intangible tax. All these charges are a percentage of the loan. There are charges on all closings for the recording of the paperwork, sometimes a charge for an amortization schedule, new loans require a new survey and an appraisal. There are also charges for setting up an escrow account. An escrow account is a sum of the buyer's money from which the lender, each year, as the bills become due, pays the taxes, the insurance policy (yearly), and PMI (yearly also). When there is an escrow account, you will also (at least in Georgia) pay at closing, three months extra each of taxes, insurance, and PMI/MIP—extra!..It amounts to a down payment on your next year's insurance policies (hazard and PMI/MIP,) which I will explain. A word about intangible tax: I call this tax the Insipid tax! It is a tax on the loan. In Georgia the intangible tax is $1.50 for each $500 borrowed or percentages of $500, in loans amounting to $2,000 or more, and with a payoff longer than two years. Can you imagine? Poor guy had to borrow money to buy a home and the State taxes him on his loan. If you borrow $2,001 from your mother, you owe the state $4.50! Would you like to know how we got this tax?... One fine day in the halls of congress, they were wondering what in the world they could tax us on...They wanted more money to spend. One fellow said "I just lent a guy $30,000. Let's tax loans! Some shouted "You can't TOUCH that! There was silence in congress. "CAN'T TOUCH...can't touch... So they called the tax INTANGIBLE TAX. We need to get rid of <u>ALL</u> of 'em, we also need TERM LIMITS!

If a person's down payment is at least 20%, the banks don't charge, at closing, some of the regular charges. For example, there is usually no escrow account. You pay your taxes, insurance yourself when the bills arrive. There is no foreclosure insurance (PMI), remember? The 80% loan is considered the safest against foreclosure. The bank assumes that if you have that much money to put down—20%--that you will be able to pay your bills yourself. My FHA loan had an escrow account. Thank Goodness for that. With four kids, wife, mother-in-law, three dogs (remember, Surely, Goodness, and Mercy?), one cat and a parakeet, don't know if I could have come up with the tax bill, or the insurance bill. Some of my customers request an escrow account although they have paid down 20%. The only negative thing is that we don't get any interest on that account as we should get. Write your congressman. The PMI (foreclosure insurance) benefits the lender. The standard PMI all over America is based on 2 ½% of your loan. Some slickee banks self insure and will try to charge more than the regular PMI company (national). They tried to charge my kids PMI of 7% at a closing, saying that being fresh out of college, student loans, etc., that my son-in-law was a bad risk. I told my kids "We are leaving!" We went to another bank who was delighted to make the home loan, with no PMI. My son-in-law had just finished his medical studies and was entering practice as a radiologist. The first bank was a rip-off, the following bank saw a great new customer. The first bank also tried to charge 9% interest. The second bank gave him 7%. I recommend, as already stated, shopping banks before you sign anything.

 Are you with me so far? Why do they charge three extra months of taxes, Ins., and PMI/MIP? If you close on the first day of any month, your first house payment will be the very next first of that next month. Your payment will include the one-twelfth of Ins., taxes, and PMI, which goes into the escrow account each month. Since you will only have made eleven payments, there will not be enough (twelve) payments to be able to pay the bill—ergo from the escrow account. If you close on the second, thirty-first....any day but the first day of the month, your very first payment comes on (skip a month) the first of the third month. Example: close on December 2. Your first payment will be on the first of February. You will have made only eleven payments by the anniversary of your closing. Taxes, insurance and PMI, could have gone up. That is the reason for the extra months' payments at closing, to be able to have enough and to cover any increase in prices. Things tend to go up! Georgia requires (allows) three months' extra payments at closing.

When some people see their closing statement and the disclosure shows that they are paying 9% interest—they signed up for 7%!, they hit the ceiling. Their agent didn't warn them. They can be assured that they will be paying 7% for thirty years, not 9%. The 9% is simply the disclosure, required at closing, that the bank is making a profit of 9% in the long run—the origination fee, any discount points, anything that generates profit for the bank. When Martha sees that their first payment is, counting this month, three months away! "Gawlee, Ralph, we don't have to make a payment the first month! Not. If you close on the second or any other day except the first, you must pay pre-paid interest through the rest of that closing month—including closing day. It is called "pre-paids." The only time in America we pay interest before using the money is at closings on the second, etc. When you make a house payment in America, say, February 1, you are paying last month's interest—January's. We always pay in arrears. I used to think that on February 1, I was caught up. Not. I had just paid the January payment. Enough said.

At closing you are paying for an insurance policy (hazard insurance) to cover loss—fire, etc. A tip for sellers is to not cancel the homeowner's insurance policy until you move into your new home. If you are moving to Texas from Georgia, closing was this morning, your furniture is on the truck, and on the way to Texas the truck wrecks and burns up, your furniture is covered. There is a Georgia state exam question for students asking "When should the seller cancel his homeowner's policy, the day of closing, or the day after closing? The answer is the day after closing. Of course, if the closing is at four o'clock and the house burns down at eleven o'clock, before closing, everything is lost if he cancelled the policy the day of closing. That is a very bad question! He should wait for cancellation until he moves into his new home where his <u>new</u> policy will take over.

For the student and teacher, here is a way to figure how many months of taxes need to be collected at closing (in Georgia always at least 3 months). I said at least 3 months taxes. In some states, Georgia included, the fiscal year begins on July 1. That's the day that taxes are due to be paid, the whole twelve months. You are paying six months late and six months early on that date. I know! You are saying "Well, our tax bill comes in October." Mine too. However, the taxes are paid on July 1! If you close on June 1, your first payment falls on July 1. That payment contains only one month's taxes. You are missing eleven! They will collect fourteen! That gives you enough along with your first payment plus three (fifteen).

Here's my invention/formula: Textbooks give you a schematic beginning with January (first month) under which is an 8. They continue: February has a 9 under it. March, a 10, and so on until you get to 15. Then the schematic continues with September, under which is a 4. Confusing, eh? Here is my invention/schematic: SON—4, 5, 6. Called SON four, five, six. I begin with the month with the lowest number under it, September. September has a 4 under it, October, a 5, November, a 6, and continue to August which has a 15. If your <u>FIRST PAYMENT</u> begins in December, look under the D (December) and find a 7. They will collect from the buyer, 7 months' taxes if he closes on November 1 or October 2 through 31. SON 4, 5, 6:

S	O	N	D	J	F	M	A	M	J	J	A
4	5	6	7	8	9	10	11	12	13	14	15

Remember that these months are <u>NOT</u> the closing month, but the month of first payment. There is one exception to the SON—4, 5, 6 rule. If you close <u>ON</u> July 1, there will be twelve months' taxes in the kitty at the end of your first payment year, and so you are only required to pay the three (remember?) extra months of taxes at closing.

One final assist to students, teachers and lawyers is Art Yorra's Schematic. I've told you about Art. Great teacher! Every time I have to prorate, I draw this schematic. It is infallible. It is a picture of closing and it is so easy to do. First of all, proration means to give the seller his due/charges and also give the same to the buyer. Everyone pays his own way. No one pays for anybody else unless they agreed to do so:

```
           Closing Date
MTD: _____I_____
YTD: _____I_____
```

The vertical line is closing date. That date belongs to the seller. After MTD, I always put the closing date. In this exercise the closing date is Dec. 8, so I place the 8:

```
           Dec. 8th
MTD: ___8__I_____
YTD: _____I_____
```

So far this month there have been 8 days. Tomorrow starts the buyer's time. Since December has thirty-one days, that leaves 23 days to go in the right quadrant:

```
           Dec. 8th
MTD: ___8__I__23___
YTD: _____I_____
```

At the bottom, YTD means Year To Date. Since January 1, and including today, there have been 342 days:

James C. Clinkscales

Dec. 8th
MTD: ___8__I__23____
YTD: __342_I_____

Beginning tomorrow there are 23 days left this year:

Dec. 8th
MTD: ___8__I__23____
YTD: __342_I__23____

We prorate always on a daily basis monthly and yearly. If the seller pays his loan off today, at closing he will also owe eight days' interest (loan times interest rate, divided by 365 days, times 8). The reason he owes 8 days' interest is that he hasn't made the January payment yet, in which he pays interest for December, remember? Don't forget Leap years. Those years divisible by four are leap years and contain <u>366</u> days. I told you earlier that closing date belongs to the seller. This interest is called <u>accrued</u> interest.

Since this closing is on the eight day of the month, the buyer will pay pre-paid interest of 23 days. Remember? If the closing had been on the first day of the month, there would be no pre-paid interest. He would pay interest for December on January 1. Here his <u>first payment due month</u> is February. Remember? The only time in America we pay interest before using the money is when we close not on the first day of the month.

If the seller is selling a rented house (a tenant is living there), he owes the buyer 23 days' rent money. After midnight tonight, the buyer will be the new landlord and should receive the rent that has already been paid to the seller. If taxes hadn't been paid, the seller would owe to the buyer 342 days' taxes. Since (in Georgia) taxes were paid back on July 1 for the entire year, the buyer owes back to the seller those 23 days at the bottom of the schematic—proration, keeping it fair. Thanks, again, Art!

Do you have a teacher still living? Is there a teacher that you remember and perchance something he/she taught you, or had an influence? Before it's too late, go say thank you. It would be so much appreciated. I have told Art. He is alone now and spends his time traveling in his motorized camper. Happy trails, Art!

Well, Buckaroos, Gentle Readers, and Cheetah Chasers, I hope that somewhere among these pages, you find yourself a Cheetah or two. Ease over into that left lane. Agents, if you make a mistake, it will be unintentional, and if you are speeding in the left lane fast enough, the mistake, if it ever surfaces, you will be well on down the road. It has been a pleasure, being able to tell you this stuff. Agents, keep up with and take notes as you travel toward "Point Z," and as you invent more Ways to buy a house, write them down! One day you will write the next book. Don't take so long though. This one took thirty-six years to write. Not. It took me that long to learn and polish these ideas. I have told you about several Cheetah Catchers and their methods. Some people probably thought what they did couldn't be done. Some things are just humanly impossible. Yeah? Back when I was young, it was humanly impossible to run one mile in less than four minutes. That was the truth. That was it. Well, in May of 1954, Roger Bannister of Britain ran the mile in three minutes 59.4 seconds at Oxford, England. Remember up until then, it couldn't be done. The very next month, on June 21, John Lundy, from New Zealand ran it in three minutes 58 seconds. Since then, the record has been broken seventeen more times. The last time was on September 5, 1993. Morrocan Hicham El Guerrouj beat Bannister's record by more than fifteen seconds! Let no one tell you "It can't be done." However, you won't break any records by just doing your best. You've got to do that something! Every day! Never mind what the truth is. Read your list. Do something. Everyone does his best but <u>you</u> should do <u>Something</u>!

    I just received an e-mail....Before I tell you about that e-mail, let me remind you what a fantastic, and I mean Fantastic, world we live in! Old hat, now, but I have a little "tie clasp" (I-pod) that has no moving parts, just a tie-clasp. My daughter installed (downloaded) thirteen of my favorite CDs onto it. I can listen to stereophonic sound just by plugging into it! What a world we have! Also, things are changing. There is this kid who looks into the mirror and an old guy is staring back at him! But, it's the same Kid looking in the mirror! Don't ever grow up! Now, the e-mail: The e-mail I received from a friend is one with Jim Reeves singing "May The Good Lord Bless And Keep You." All the words of that song are my wishes for you. Now, the only thing left to say, except that I hope to hear from you and your successes, is what the great, late Red Skelton used to say at the end of his every show: "May God Bless."

www.ingramcontent.com/pod-product-compliance
Lightning Source LLC
Chambersburg PA
CBHW030818180526
45163CB00003B/1338